PUBLIC SECTOR

As the title of the book itself suggests, public enterprises were good in the early stages of development after independence. But as it gathered steam, it picked several bad practices on the way leading to inefficiency, political interference, nepotism and poor management leading to some becoming unviable and unsustainable. With the liberalisation in 1991, some changed to take on competition and even improved its efficiency but many collapsed as they were good only in monopolistic situation. Some, which were inefficient even in socialistic era deteriorated further. Successive government in post liberalisation era has attempted to improve the functioning but mustered courage to take bold decisions to privatise or close down especially unviable units. This cost the exchequer heavily. Vajpayee government did attempt some strategic sale. There were some good and bad experiences in his efforts. It is only after Prime Minister Narendra Modi came to power in 2014 a serious attempt has been made to carry out long pending reforms of public enterprises. It had taken more than five years for him to work out a clear-cut strategy hive-off all public enterprises in non-strategic areas and limit the number to four PSUs in strategic sectors. This is a refreshing development. Clearer picture will emerge only when details are spelt out.

PUBLIC SECTOR

The Good, The Bad, The Ugly

K R Sudhaman

HAR-ANAND
PUBLICATIONS PVT LTD

HAR-ANAND PUBLICATIONS PVT LTD
E-49/3, Okhla Industrial Area, Phase-II, New Delhi-110020
Tel.: 41603490
E-mail: info@haranandbooks.com/haranand@rediffmail.com
Shop online at: www.haranandbooks.com

Published by Ashok Gosain and Ashish Gosain for
Har-Anand Publications Pvt Ltd

Printed in India at Vinayak Offset

Dedicated to my parents

Kamala

&

K V Ramakrishnan

Preface

Public Sector is a much maligned word these days as the flavor now is privatization. It is unfortunate that we forget the yeomen service it has done to the economic development of India. If profit is the motive or commercial consideration is the objective then public sector surely fails the test. That is precisely the reason why we try to misjudge its valuable contribution to the nation building. It's regrettable that we judge its performance from this angle though its contribution to the economy is manifold. The objective of public sector is totally different. Public sector enters area where private sector does not want to tread. It has several social objectives to fulfill. Sometimes it could be regional development, sometimes it is to bring about price stabilization and deal with shortages. It has a role in checking black marketing. Sometimes it could be a case of huge investment and long gestation period and private sector does not have the wherewithal. Sometimes it has social objectives to be met and perhaps push up employment. Sometimes it has a role in preventing job losses as was the case in nationalization of sick textile mills. So if public sector performance is to be judged, it has to be judged from the point of whether it has fulfilled the objectives for which it had been set up. If that is the yardstick then, most of the public enterprises performance would be above par. Otherwise too many Public enterprises have performed much better than private enterprises. In fact, World over, public sector is not considered efficient. This is because Public enterprises boards are never truly Independent because government owns and controls them, The board always functions with one hand tied behind its back as the master that is, government, scarcely know how to run it efficiently. Ideally government should not be in business of running business but sometimes the situation may compel it to run business. The main problem therefore is not public sector but the fact is there is no exit policy for it to get out when it has fulfilled its objectives or outlived its utility. Many public enterprises were set up to deal with difficult situation at a particular point of time and once it is done, it should automatically exit but that does not happen making them sick and patently unviable. To cite a few examples, Modern Bread was set up in various cities to deal with bread and food shortages. Once the era of shortages was over and many private bakeries have mushroomed, it should have automatically exited. But that did not happen. Of course Modern Bread was sold off much later after running into huge loss. Highly labour intensive private textile mills became sick due to lack of modernization and investment. They had to be nationalized to protect employment at a time when jobs were scarce. Since there was no exit policy and inadequate labour reforms, government could not get rid of these nationalized mills when industrial activity boomed, Vested interests of trade unions of this redundant labour prevailed because of their political clout and as a result the nationalized mills became a burden. Likewise Air India and Indian Airlines were formed by taking over private airlines which was the right move at that point of time as World over airlines were in public sector because of the huge investment involved and security considerations. But when skies were opened up to the private sector and many government airlines were privatized, government failed to off-load Air India, which at one time was top class airlines. Prime Minister Narendra Modi has now decided to take the bull by the horn and privatise many or most of the public enterprises, which had outlived its utility. This book while highlighting the merit of public sector it analyses why public enterprises should get out of non core business and selectively in core business as well to inject competition and efficiency and garner resources through stake sale for developmental activities. There is no merit in the argument that off-loading public enterprises is like selling family silver to pay the grocers' bill. Family silver is meant to bail out during rainy days. India did pledge its gold to prevent default in global payments. It did get its gold back and perhaps a little more when the situation improved. Modi is certainly on the right track as there is need to unlock value of public enterprises which is over Rs 10 lakh crore. This will also ensure that enterprises are run efficiently to leapfrog in economic development. This book make an attempt to analyze various good, bad and ugly aspects of public enterprises.

K R SUDHAMAN

Contents

CHAPTER 1

A Brief History of Public Enterprises in India at the Dawn of Independence

A lot has been written about public enterprises in this country. They are mostly critical appraisal of public enterprises highlighting their failures rather than the good they have done to the economy from time to time. Critical appraisal is good as it helps in overcoming the deficiencies in the functioning. But world over it is public enterprises that laid the foundation for economic development, more so after the World War and the great depression of the 1930s. India is no exception. Our founding fathers took a conscious decision to adopt a socialistic pattern of development in the initial years that utilised public enterprises as a means of economic development. It is not that they did not have faith in private enterprises. But policy planners at that time felt rapid economic development cannot be achieved in a poor country like India with large population without state playing a key role in the transformation. Also in impoverished economy, private sector did not have the financial muscle. Profit is critical for capital formation but in an impoverished economy large investment can come only from the state and that too when there is long gestation period and social objectives to be fulfilled side by side with industrial development.

NEHRU'S CONTRIBUTION TO PUBLIC ENTERPRISES DEVELOPMENT

Despite the pitfalls of public sector in the early stages of development, India certainly owes to its visionary leaders particularly Pandit Jawaharlal Nehru, first Prime Minister, for laying the strong foundation for industrial development. India's development process may not have been rapid as in some miracle countries of East and South East Asia. But countries with large population cannot built upon without strong base as any collapse will be more disasterous than smaller countries. China too adopted socialistic pattern in the early stages of development. Its rapid growth began only after it opened up the economy after state owned companies laid a strong foundation.

There is therefore no validity in the criticism India's growth process was slow until it opened up the economy. True the growth rate was not rapid but certainly it was steady and there was no major economic shock excepting when it was induced by external factors or due to drought. This set the right platform for uplift of the vast majority of people. But for state playing a critical role in distribution of wealth and production of goods and services India will certainly not be where it is today even though India may not achieved double digit growth on a sustained basis like China for decades. One swallow cannot make summer. No economy in the world barring China has achieved double digit growth on a sustained basis. Not even countries like Germany, Japan or South Korea, considered to be miracle economies in the post world war era. If India is in a take off stage to be the fastest growing economy until corona virus shook the world forcing the global economy to go on a tail spin. Nevertheless, India still has the potential to be among the fastest growing economies once the recovery begins most probably in the second half of the 2020. Of course the World economy is not going to be same but it is going to be India that will lead the way and certainly not China with many multinationals looking to move out of China and are keen to create an alternative or a second global manufacturing hub. Here, it is the foundation laid by public enterprises particularly in the development of heavy industries and infrastructure in the early years of independence, will play a critical role. With huge land parcels at their disposal, it is public enterprises that is going to call the shots in setting up joint ventures with multinational companies. It may also help in unlocking value of public enterprises. The central government public enterprises are valued over Rs 10 lakh crore and can provide much needed push to public spending in creating world class infrastructure in the country, which currently has huge deficit.

There may have been shortcomings but running public enterprises only on commercial lines with profit as the sole motive is not possible in the early stages of development of a country, that too when the nation has adopted democracy. Democracy is a slow process of polity but brings in political and economic stability and India is a role model to the World in this regard.

PROFIT CANNOT BE ONLY MOTIVE OF PUBLIC ENTERPRISES

Profit cannot be the only motive as in a free market economy in an impoverished country where nearly half the population did not have the means even for two square meals a day in 1947. If India has come a long way from a GDP of mere Rs 94 billion in 1950 to close to 3 trillion until coronovirus and lock down hit the economy, it is because state owned companies played a key role. It provided the much needed hand holding to enable the economy to stand on its own feet. Also it created quite a bit of infrastructure in remote area, by virtually building townships around public enterprises. It also helped in the development of small scale industry clusters through ancillarisation of its production chain.

There has always been a critical appraisal of the performance of public enterprises. It is frequently debated in Parliament with opposition pouncing on government to tone up their functioning. State enterprises are of three types—One is departmentally owned and run like the Railways and Posts. Second is units owned by state governments including state electricity boards and state road transport corporations. Third is companies or corporations run by the central government.

India's progress during the last seven decades and more could not have happened without public sector despite the fact there were several loss making organisations. It is really unfortunate that performance of public enterprises are measured by the same yardstick as private enterprises. Commercial considerations cannot be sole guiding principles for public enterprises. This does not mean that state-owned companies should not be free from government, bureaucratic and procedural shackles. Also state owned companies are expected to achieve commercial goals which are in conflict with maximisation of profit. The so-called autonomy of public enterprises is often a casualty because of political interference Many a times social objectives have to be fulfilled at the cost of profit. Public enterprises are assigned different tasks at different points of time. Also it varied from industry to industry. Some public enterprises are set up only to bring about price stability even at the cost of commercial viability. Some are set up to correct regional imbalances resulting in high cost of operation. So clear cut objectives, appointment of competent and professional managers and technocrats and greater autonomy will help in improving efficiency and governance of public enterprises.

Some studies show that private enterprises are more corrupt than public enterprises. The only difference is that failures in public enterprises are magnified and overstated. They often come under public scrutiny unlike in private enterprises where there are more opportunity to suppress. Critics always see performance of public enterprises through a microscope while underplaying the failures of private enterprises. Everything is not hunky dory with public enterprises, but lately it has become fashion to criticise public sector ignoring all the good work they have done particularly after liberalisation of the economy. Of course there is a need for reforming public enterprises and hiving off from some of the areas where public enterprises have outlived its utility. There is also need to inject competition and end the monopolistic stranglehold of public enterprises in some sectors.

But private sector can only complement and supplement public enterprises. It is worthwhile to consider offloading public sector companies in non core areas as part of the strategy to tone up their functioning. But the investments in public enterprise are huge and are in critical areas and hence any privatisation has to be done in a calibrated manner as well as on a case-by-case basis. There are great examples of success as well as failures in public enterprises just as in private enterprises. Improving public enterprises functioning has to be a constant endeavour While it may be worthwhile to consider standardisation of products in some cases to achieve economies of scale in a poor country, one size fits all solutions to ills of public enterprises should be avoided. It is regrettable that critics see performance of public enterprises with a microscope while underplaying the failures of private enterprises. It however does not mean privatisation of public enterprises should not be attempted as some of them like Food Corporation of India has outlived its utility. But at that point of time it was critical to set up a monolothic organisation like FCI in an era of foodgrain shortage. Now India does not live in an era of food shortages and hence FCI, which has served its purpose, could be dismantled in a phased manner and reoriented to serve present day needs.

Public Enterprises Existed in Ancient Times Too

State owned companies as means for wealth creation and improving governance was recognised even during ancient times. There is a mention of state owned companies in Kautalya's Arthashastra during the Maurya period dating back to 300 BC.

Countries like India and China with large agrarian unskilled illiterate population in 1950s, government could not have left everything to private sector where profit is the sole objective. Even if private sector fulfilled certain social objectives, profit was always the primary objective and nation building was never the main objective.

In various stages of history Indian rulers have taken to public enterprises as a means of sustainable development particularly in manufacturing and items of mass consumption like salt and transport as these have direct bearing on governance. History has recorded prevalence of state owned companies during Gupta and Moghul periods. Several kingdoms turned to state ownership where strategic interests are involved.

Economists, thinkers and philosophers have come out with different theories time to time on ownership of capital and labour. While Adam Smith preferred free market Karl Marx felt state should be the main actor for economic growth. Both had merits and demerits. The world has seen collapse of extremely left oriented socialist pattern of economic development in the erstwhile Soviet Union as well as the free market capitalist economy as demonstrated by the most recent 2008 US financial crisis. The global financial meltdown was triggered by collapse of Lehman Brothers resulting in a massive bailout by the state.

MIXED ECONOMY A BETTER OPTION TO SOCIALISM OR CAPITALISM

India's founding fathers had a vision not to blindly follow the extreme left or right philosophy as history has shown neither worked fully. In hind sight, analysing the chain of events that had taken place in the economy the middle path of mixed economy was the most appropriate for a poor country like India, which had to develop from a scratch after 200 years of colonial rule that pushed down India's economy. India which accounted for 23 per cent of World GDP in 18th century accounted for a mere 4 per cent when Britishers left India in 1947 after dividing the country into two.

After Independence India did not want to stifle the individual entrepreneurial skills. At the same the state did not want to distance itself in the economic development of the country where there is a large scale hunger, poverty, scarcity of resources for industrial development in a predominantly agrarian economy.

The 19th century Industrial Revolution in Europe and United States had very little impact on India which under subjugation of British Rule. Britain benefited from India as it became a major source of raw material particularly cotton and Jute for British mills, coal and other minerals of their Industry. It also ensured well developed Indian handicrafts were systematically killed while promoting textiles from Manchester and other manufactured goods from England. Some industries like sugar, tea, jute and textiles were developed in India to suit the British masters but certainly large scale industries were not developed excepting infrastructure like Railways, Posts and Telegraph, basically to serve their interests like movement of troops, communication and certainly not for the economic development of interior and rural parts of the country. Ports were developed in areas where it was needed for them. This is one of the reasons that the Railways and irrigation system developed by the Britishers in India did not act as a catalyst for industrial progress of the country.

The two world wars and the great depression of 1930s made the situation worse for India coupled with the Bengal famine of 1942. To take the fledgling economy out of the crisis situation, the founding fathers decided on a planned development which provided a dominant role to public enterprises.

The Industrial Policy Resolution of 1948, the first in independent India laid the roadmap for the mixed economic development that resolved to establish a social order where justice and equality of opportunity shall be assured to all people. Even before Independence, the congress party, which was in the forefront of India's freedom struggle, set up a national planning committee under the chairmanship of Jawaharlal Nehru, for industrialisation and agriculture development emboldened by the party's success in 1937 elections in which it got majority in eight of the 11 provinces in the country at that time. Then came People's plan by M N Roy of Indian Federation of Labour, which proposed a Rs 15,000 crore investment plan over 15 years. With emphasis being on agriculture, eight top industrialists of country came out with what had come to be known as Bombay Plan that gave more importance to industrial development. The Planning committee too prepared an industrial policy statement for post World War ll reconstruction. All these got superseded by the Industrial Policy Resolution of 1948, which for the first time clearly demarcated the role of public and private sector in industrial development.

The response of private sector to the industrial development was lukewarm with Prime Minister Nehru adopting socialistic pattern of development. Adopting socialistic pattern on the Soviet model has now become a debatable issue. In hind sight it could be argued it was not very appropriate as it led to inspector-licence-permit-quota raj. Nevertheless this pattern of development laid the foundation of industrial development through public enterprises. There was lurking fear of nationalisation of private companies, which was however unfounded. Nor public enterprises made big strides in the initial years as the stress was in agriculture, particularly in the back drop of Bengal famine of 1942 in which millions of people died due to starvation. The green revolution in the 1960s ensured starvation deaths was the thing of the past. Incidentally private sector dominated agriculture as farm land is usually owned by families and individuals.

Government too did not lay emphasis on industrial development in the first five-year plan that began in 1951, which came to be known as a plan to stablise India's agriculture giving thrust to expand irrigation to reduce dependence of farming on the vagaries of weather. As a result India had just five public enterprises with an investment of just Rs 29 crore in 1951. Though India adopted socialistic pattern of development with special emphasis for public enterprises, the much needed push came only in the second five year plan that too after the formulation of the 1956 Industrial Policy Resolution. The industrial policy was reformulated to address the concerns of private sector which were apprehensive government may nationalise their industries at the drop of a hat.

The second five-year plan, which is based on Mahalanobis growth model that prescribed setting up of heavy industries as a strategy for economic development and job creation. A close friend and adviser of Jawaharlal Nehru, Prof P C Mahalanobis based his strategy on the original Feldman-Mahalanobis model of economic development. The Neo-Marxist model was developed independently by G A Feldman Soviet economist in 1928 and Mahalanobis, Indian Statistician, in 1953. The model envisaged huge investments in building capacity in the production of capital goods first so as to move towards building up domestic consumption goods. Feldman first introduced this idea in the Soviet plan in 1928. He was working as an economist in Gosplan, Soviet Planning commission. Mahalnobis, who as key economist in the Indian Planning Commission implemented the model in the second five year plan which was followed right up to fifth five year plan, when it was abandoned by the Janata Government, the first non congress government headed by Prime Minister Morarji Desai. This model was terminated in March 1978, one year before the completion of full five years of the fifth plan as there was change in government's economic policy. History does not record any evidence to suggest that Mahalanobis knew Feldman's approach and that's why the economic model is named after both the persons. The basic approach of the model is that to achieve rapid long-term growth, the major part of the plan outlay has to spend on building basic heavy industries. There is one major criticism of the model is that it did not pay attention to increasing savings in the country, essential to step up capital formation. Mahalanobis was of the view that in a closed economy, the rate of real capital formation depended upon the capacity to produce capital goods and certainly not on the savings of the economy. This philosophy was justified in those times when there was a lot of emphasis on self-reliance and there was protectionist tendency world over particularly after the second World War, when most economies were in the process of rebuilding.

The 1956 Industrial Policy Resolution formulated in this background set the stage for glorious development of public enterprises. This socialistic pattern of development was necessitated by the slow industrialisation of India between 1948 and 1956. The private sector did not mobilise adequate resources for investment during this period and not much was forthcoming from the government as its emphasis was on development of agriculture at that point of time. So armed with the 1956 Industrial Policy Resolution, the government took direct responsibility for industrial development. With Government's resolve to push heavy industries, steel plants, fertiliser plants, railway coach factory, power plants, heavy electricals and chemicals came up in the public sector. The second plan industrial investment targets were achieved. An outlay of Rs 938 crore was provided for large scale industries and Rs 187 crore for development of small scale industries was provided and the economy achieved 6.6 per cent industrial growth. The government also nationalised life insurance industry in India. Life Insurance Corporation of India was founded through the passage of LIC Act in 1956 that nationalised private insurance industry in India.

Nearly 250 insurance companies and provident societies were merged to create the state owned Life Insurance Corporation. The 1956 Industrial Policy Resolution led to nationalisation of life insurance business as it was among the 17 sectors, which was envisaged to be under state control under the policy. This also subsequently helped in providing long-term funding for infrastructure development, which was mostly done by the government. The banking industry, crucial for development, also had some churning with the conversion of Imperial Bank into State Bank of India through an act of Parliament in 1955-56. The Imperial Bank was formed in 1921 by merging three Presidency Banks in Calcutta, Bombay and Madras set up in the 19th century. This was considered to be the major bank in India then and today State Bank of India is the largest bank in the country and among the top 25 Asian banks. In 1959 eight banks in as many princely states were taken over to form eight subsidiary banks of SBI providing more financial muscle to the Government to economic development. Now these eight subsidiary banks have been merged into State Bank of India making the bank that much more bigger. Still none of the Indian banks are in the top ten or top 25 banks in World. But there are many Chinese banks in that list.

With government laying the foundation for the development of state-owned companies, it has only grown covering many spheres of activity as the economic situation demanded. Public sector in both centre and states played crucial role and even after liberalisation of the economy in 1991, it is the state-owned companies that is in forefront of development. Today when there is crying need to push investment to kickstart the sagging economy, it is the public sector, which are taking giant steps to revive investment cycle. Private sector companies are still in wait and watch mode and are afraid of testing water, a job that has been left to state-owned companies.

Greater autonomy, professionalisation of management, improving efficiency and governance will have to be a constant endeavour. In a dynamic world changes will have to happen. Of course it is happening but it will always be debated weather it is adequate or not. The contribution to infrastructure development, defence production and heavy industries, Public enterprises have done yeomen service during the last seven decades and more. On the positive side if India is nearly a $ 3 trillion economy and poised to leap frog in the coming years and decades to become third largest economy after United States and China, contribution of public enterprises cannot be ignored.

CHAPTER 2

Public Enterprises are Modern Temples of India

India's first Prime Miniser Pandit Jawaharlal Nehru said when he inaugurated the first major multi-purpose dam built in independent India at Bhakra Nangal that "As I walked round the (Bhakra-Nangal) site I thought that these days the biggest temple and mosque and Gurdwara is the place where man works for the good of mankind. Which place can be greater than this, this Bhakra-Nangal, where thousands and lakhs of men have worked, have shed their blood and sweat and laid down their lives as well? Where can be a greater and holier place than this, which we can regard as higher?"

This aptly sums up the fact that such huge projects aimed at social uplift of people by bringing about agricultural and industrial revolution in India surely needed to be worshipped. In the early stages of development in independent India, such projects were mostly in the public sector.

TWO HUNDRED YEARS OF BRITISH RULE

The 200 years of British rule had several negative developments on Indian economy. It was highly exploitative. So the first task of the new Indian government was to rebuild the economy in a manner that is non-disruptive and that too without impinging upon democratic norms. India inherited a crippled economy and hence the thrust has to be on developing both agriculture and industry. The country's infrastructure too required massive upgrade. India had power generating capacity of mere 2000 Mw in 1950. Today India has come a long way at nearly 4 lakh Mw power generation capacity. Power is a critical input for both industry and agriculture. Increasing per capita consumption of electricity is critical as it is one of the indicators of development. India is still far behind world average. Only recently, India fulfilled the task of electrifying all the 6.3 lakh villages in India. Considering that the country is large, resources are inadequate and terrain difficult in some parts, its no small achievement. Prime Minister Narendra Modi during his first five years of his rule accomplished this task by electifying all the remaining 19,000 unelectrified villages in the country. Modi government rightly took the credit but all the previous governments have contributed to it through sustained effort in ensuring all the 6.3 lakh villages in the country has electricity. It is however debatable if this could have been achieved earlier instead of accompalishing it in 70 years after independence. Still it goes to the credit of Indian government for having this important task fulfilled better late than never.

BRITISH LEAVE A SHATTERED ECONOMY AT THE TIME OF INDEPENDENCE

The shattered and impoverished Indian Economy left by Britishers had to start with building such basic infrastructure, which also meant the need to build basic and heavy industries so that India became self reliant so that its dependence on developed nations for import of strategic equipment came down in a phased manner. The idea was to concentrate first on building import substituting heavy industries that formed the backbone for sustainable industrial and agricultural development. There was a realisation that without adequate power, steel, cement and other core industries, India cannot march towards industrial development.

The first Industrial Policy Resolution of 1948 prepared in this backdrop and based on the experience on the ground, needed to be tweaked as the private sector could not fully rise to the occasion nor did it have the wherewithal or the resources for huge investments in vital and core sectors. This led to formulation of 1956 Industrial policy Resolution, which went whole hog in the development of Public Enterprises. The policy was formulated after widespread debate in the country with a clear and emphatic decision to adopt socialistic pattern of development.

With concerted effort of the first Indian Government and through continuous learning, more and more public sector projects were taken up. From a mere five public enterprises at the beginning of first five year plan in 1951, the number of public sector enterprises grew to 47 and investments jumping up over 30 times to nearly Rs 1000 crore that is Rs 959 crore to be precise by the end of the Second Five Year plan in 1961, which was a big amount in those days prices. The socialistic pattern of development, which took a firm root by then and Public Sector got into production of several major basic and heavy industries providing the much needed foundation to boost industrial growth.

Job creation was also a priority and hence labour intensive technology was adopted as the country was endowed with abundant cheap labour. As many as 24 lakh people were recruited during this period in public enterprises. The public sector has grown since then and today there are around 290 central PSUs with investment of over Rs 10 lakh crore. There are about 1000 state PSUs as well with investment of nearly Rs 4 lakh crore in 28 states and nine union territories. The turnover of Central public sector contributed around 22 per cent of GDP. The State PSEs contribution to state GSDP too was significant.

FIVE PSUs IN 1951

The five public sector undertakings in 1951 included Damodar Valley Corporation in power generation, Indian Telephone Industries to manufacture telephones and telephone exchanges, Indian Rare Earth Limited and NEPA. All of these were basic industries to push infrastructure development.

In the early part of 1950s more public sector undertaking were set up including Oil and Natural Gas Commission, now known as Oil and

Natural Gas Corporation Ltd., Neyveli Lignite Corporation Ltd., Hindustan Machine Tools Ltd., Bharat Electronics Ltd., Hindustan antibiotics Ltd., Hindustan insecticides Ltd. and Hindustan Shipyards Ltd. They were into oil production, power generation, electronics and ship building. There were also companies like Mazagaon Docks Ltd. and Balmer Lawrie Ltd., Andrew Yule Ltd. which were set up prior to independence and they became part of public sector family subsequently. This indicated the pattern of investment in Public Sector, basically in areas where private sector would not enter because of low return.

Indian government and then the ruling party felt industrialisation alone will provide the much needed jobs for people migrating from rural areas. Agriculture however had to be given equal importance as productivity had to be increased substantially to provide food security to the people, now over 1.3 billion.

With fragmentation of land, the migrating workforce from 6.3 lakh villages in the country can be absorbed only through industrialisation that called for massive investment in infrastructure, urbanisation and heavy industry. This was necessary to facilitate growth of small industries in private sector to compliment public sector in the industrialisation of the country.

India's 1948 Industrial Policy Resolution was originally aimed at bridging disparity among human beings and regions through rapid industrialization. The strategy was to pursue policy of mixed economy with top priority to public sector. This strategy was aimed at ensuring state played a key role while not undermining individual entrepreneurial efforts.

The government visualised a democratic economy with liberal approach. The government did not want India to be regimented, rigid and dictatorial as in communist countries. The Industrial policy was tailored to encourage individual liberty, talent and ability particularly in a country with vast population and diverse culture, language, regions, castes and religion. The opinion in the government was that If people are to be uplifted from extreme poverty, there is no choice but for state to become a major player in industrial progress without scuttling individual efforts. This is because private sector cannot be expected to put in their money until they gained thrust of the government.

Despite being left of centre approach, India, did not adopt extreme form of socialism as in communist China or the erstwhile Soviet Union. Lessons were however drawn particularly from the Soviet Union on planned economic development for large and heavy industries development while giving importance to the growth of small scale industries.

The then government recognized that public and private sectors will have to play complementary and supplementary role, but the State will play lead role. There were also right of the Centre view from leaders like C Rajagopalachari, the first and the only Indian Governor-General, that over-centralization will lead to License-Inspector-Permit-quota Raj.

CONSENSUS ON SOCIALISTIC PATTERN

But broad consensus prevailed in pursuing socialistic pattern, the trend world over at that time particularly after the Second World War. Only Four decades later Government embarked upon economic reforms in 1991 with an objective to dismantle licence-inspector-permitt-quota raj that came in the way of speeding up economic growth. But public sector's contribution even in changed circumstances was phenomenal as it always led from the front in the industrialisation of the country. Opening up, helped the Public Sector as well as it became more competitive and more professional. In the first four decades after independence, Public Enterprises laid the much needed foundation for Industrial development with Public Enterprises being set up in virtually important areas like banking, civil aviation, Railways, Shipbuilding, Heavy Electricals, Power Generation Equipment, Steel, Aluminum, Defence equipment, Heavy Engineering, Electronics and so on.

In the early stages of economic development the attempt should be to achieving more equitable distribution of wealth. Over concentration of wealth in the hands of few individuals had the potential danger of turning the country into a Banana Republic. History has enough evidence of this and many examples are there in Latin America and Africa. There are some in our neighborhood as well. Socialistic pattern of development in the initial stages followed by liberalisation after the economy become more matured had ensured that Industrial development was sustainable.

Some of the miracle economies in Asia, which gave preference to private sector development, witnessed major crises like the East Asian Currency meltdown in 1990s. The development pattern of mixed economy ensured India was able to weather all kinds of economic storm. Even during the green revolution of 1960s that made India self-sufficient in food grains, the public sector played an important role. Food Corporation of India set up in the mid-1960s provided much needed storage facility in the country, besides playing and important role in procurement and maintenance of buffer stocks.. With overflowing food grains stock, over three times the buffer requirement of 20 million tones, there is need for development of storage system with small stocks maintained in every nook and corner of the country.

Indian Government's thinking on economic development was articulated by Prime Minister Jawaharlal Nehru at the 1955 Congress session at Avadi, near Chennai, then known as Madras. This set the tone for making State enterprises as a pivot and engine of growth.

The then government had spent entire five years of the First Plan beginning 1951 in putting the devastated agrarian economy back on rails. The next task was to work out a blue print for a self-reliant modern economy. Initially, the emphasis was to build heavy industry so that strong foundation is laid for industrial and infrastructure development.

This made the government rework the 1948 Industrial policy Resolution in 1956. Immediately after the reformulation of industrial policy, Parliament passed Companies Act of 1956 for orderly industrial development. The Second Five Year Plan was drafted in this backdrop, which adopted Mahalanobis Model of development in which state played critical role in the development of heavy industries and infrastructure. The policy clearly encouraged public sector in all industries of basic and strategic importance so that strong foundation was built up for industrial growth The Second Five Year Plan chalked out strategy on the basis of this economic agenda to develop public enterprises in Iron, steel, coal, electricity, heavy chemicals and expand to other areas like aluminum, copper, atomic energy, and defence production.

The attempt was to make Indian people and even Government of India conscious of scientific work and the necessity for it. This also required development of human resources and hence development of institutes of higher learning like IITs and All India Institute of Medical Sciences.

The Industrial Policy Resolution 1956 classified industries in to three categories: public enterprises, mixed enterprises and private enterprises. In the first category called schedule 'A', 17 industries were reserved for public sector. Industries of basic and strategic importance requiring massive capital came under this category. The exclusive control over these industries was with the government. In the second category, schedule 'B' 12 industries were listed which will be progressively State owned. While the State will take the initiative in setting up these new undertakings, private enterprise will also have the opportunity to develop in these fields.

All the remaining industries formed third category and their development, in general, has been left open. While it was basically left to private sector to develop these industries, State can also set up any industry in this category. The State would also facilitate and encourage the development of these industries in accordance with the programmes formulated in successive five year plans.

The Industrial Policy encouraged cottage and small scale industries as well by supporting establishment of industrial estates. In this, State Enterprises contributed by encouraging ancillary industries around large PSUs, mostly in backward areas. This led to development of new townships.

The industrial policy resolution aimed at narrowing regional disparities and balanced development. There were however no watertight compartments between public and private sectors. Some PSUs obtained some of their requirements from the private sector. Some laws governing industrial relations were enacted. The entrepreneurs in public sector were asked to set an example in promoting good labour relations, an essential ingredient of socialistic pattern of development.

As far as foreign capital was concerned it was similar to 1948 Industrial Policy Resolution giving self reliance top most priority. It also favoured decentralization of authority and management of the State undertakings. Foreign collaboration were entered into by PSUs to acquire technology.

SECOND FIVE-YEAR PLAN

Armed with this economic strategy, the Second Five Year Plan beginning 1956 set India on the path of industrialization.

The First Five-Year Plan (1951-56), laid emphasis only on capacity building of existing industries such as cotton, woolen and jute textiles, cement, paper, newsprint, power-looms, medicine, paints, sugar, vanaspati (vegetable oil), chemical and engineering goods, and transport equipment.

It was the second Five-Year Plan, that laid the foundation for building heavy industries, the core of Mahalanobis growth Model for job creating development.

A statistician of repute, Prof P C Mahalanobis, based his strategy on the original Feldman-Mahalanobis model of economic development. The Neo-Marxist model was developed independently by G A Feldman, Soviet economist who worked for GOSPLAN, Soviet Planning Commission, first introduced this idea in 1928, and Mahalanobis in 1953. The model envisages huge investments in building capacity in the production of capital goods.

A great visionary Professor Prasanta Chandra Mahalanobis, who founded Indian Statistical Institute in Calcutta and this growth model was followed right up to Fifth Five-Year plan. His model was however criticized for not paying attention to increasing savings in the country, a must to raise capital formation. Mahalanobis model was abandoned by the Janata Government, the first non congress government in 1978, one year before the completion of full five years of the Fifth Plan. Janata Government wanted to give more emphasis to the development of small scale industries and not basic and heavy industries.

THE PLAN ATTEMPTED SELF-RELIANT ECONOMY

Aimed at Self-reliance in an era of protectionism, Public Sector was entrusted in the second plan the task of developing heavy industries, steel plants, fertiliser plants, railway coach factory, power plants, heavy electricals and chemicals. The Plan set an industrial investment target at Rs 938 crore for large scale industries. The outlay for development of small scale industries was Rs 187 crore, considered a substantial number that helped the economy achieve 6.6 per cent industrial growth during the plan.

NATIONALIZATION OF INSURANCE INDUSTRY

The government also nationalized life insurance industry in India during this period. Life Insurance Corporation of India was founded through the passage of LIC Act in 1956 that nationalized private insurance industry in India. Nearly 250 insurance companies and provident fund societies were merged to create the State owned Life Insurance Corporation. Life insurance business was nationalized as it was among the 17 sectors, which had to be under State control in the 1956 Industrial policy. This move helped in providing long-term funding for infrastructure development, which were mostly State owned then.

As result of the 1956 Industrial policy resolution many industries like the three steel plants at Durgapur, Rourkela and Bhillai came to be estabilished as also the heavy engineering unit at Ranchi with capacity to fabricate equipment for one million tone steel making capacity every year and also other heavy and complex machines. Heavy electrical engineering industries at Hardwar, Bhopal, Hyderabad, and Thiruchirapally were established, which according to the then Heavy Industries Minister C Subramaniam, formed spinal chord of India. This also led to creation of sufficient capacity to manufacture heavy electrical equipment for generation, transmission and distribution were created in collaboration with the erstwhile Soviet Union, United Kindgom and Czechoslavakia. Power was a basic requirement for industrialisation and rightly priority was given in the manufacture of power equipment including generators as part of public enterprises expansion.

With the establishment of public enterprises, began the process of decolonisation and strengthening of economic independence and autonomous development of the newly liberated India. The kind of public sector enterprises set up during the period ensured that public sector played significant role in the planned economic development in subsequent decades and India became a role model for many developing countries.

INSURANCE SECTOR

The Oriental Life Insurance Company, was the first company in India to offer life insurance coverage. It was established in Calcutta in 1818 and the primary target market was the Europeans based in India, and it charged Indians heftier premiums. The Hindusthan Insurance Society was formed, which later became Life Insurance Corporation. The Bombay Mutual Life Assurance Society, formed in 1870, was the first native insurance provider. Other insurance companies established in the pre-independence era included

- Postal Life Insurance (PLI) was introduced on 1 February 1884
- Bharat Insurance Company (1896)
- United India (1906)
- National Indian (1906)
- National Insurance (1906)
- Co-operative Assurance (1906)

- Hindustan Co-operatives (1907)
- Indian Mercantile
- General Assurance
- Swadeshi Life (later Bombay Life)
- Sahyadri Insurance (Merged into LIC, 1986)

In 1955, Parliamentarian *Amol Barate* raised the matter of insurance fraud by owners of private insurance agencies and India's wealthy businessmen, Ramkrishna Dalmia was sentenced to imprisonment for two years following an investigation.

LIFE INSURANCE CORPORATION OF INDIA

In the face of the insurance fraud in the private sector, LIC Act was passed in June 1956 that led to creation of Life Insurance Corporation of India, which started operation in September 1956. LIC consisted of 154 life insurance companies, 16 foreign companies and 75 provident companies.

LIC has since grown and it now contribute at least 7per cent of GDP and has a corpus of nearly $ 30 billion and employs over 25,000 people and accounted for about 450 million policies. Since opening up of the economy in 1991, LIC has only grown further taking on competition from private and foreign players. Its premium has been growing around 20 per cent annually. Now LIC is among the public enterprise where government proposed first list and start the disinvestment process. LIC is one public enterprise, which has grown and remained the leader in the sector even after Insurance sector was opened up to private players and foreign direct investment in the late 1990s and early 2000.

CONSOLIDATION OF BANKING SECTOR

The banking industry crucial for development also had some churning with the conversion of Imperial Bank into State Bank of India through an Act of Parliament in 1955-56. The Imperial Bank was formed in 1921 by merging three Presidency Banks in Calcutta, Bombay and Madras set up in the 19th century. This was considered to be the major bank in India then and today State Bank of India is the largest bank in the country and among the top 25 Asian banks. In 1959 eight banks in as many princely states were also taken over to form eight subsidiary banks of SBI providing more financial muscle to the Government. Today SBI has a turnover of over Rs 2 lakh crore and assets totaling over Rs 20 lakh crore.

State Bank of India has now become an Indian multinational, Public Sector Banking and financial services company. It has over 17,000 branches, including 190 foreign offices, making it the largest banking and financial services company in India by assets. Now State Bank of India is a regional banking behemoth and has 20 per cent market share in deposits and loans among Indian commercial banks.

SBI has acquired local banks in rescues. The first was the Bank of Bihar, which SBI acquired in 1969, together with its 28 branches. The next year SBI acquired National Bank of Lahore, which had 24 branches. Five years later, in 1975, SBI acquired Krishnaram Baldeo Bank, which had been established in 1916 in Gwalior State, under the patronage of Maharaja Madho Rao Scindia. The bank had been the *Dukan Pichadi*, a small moneylender, owned by the Maharaja. SBI acquired the Bank of Cochin, which had 120 branches. Now all the remaining associate banks have been merged into SBI to create a "mega bank" and streamline the group's operations. Two of it was first merged. They are State Bank of Saurashtra and State Bank of Indore. The others which were merged in one go by the Modi government are State Bank of Patiala, State Bank of Mysore, State Bank of Travancore, State Bank of Bikaner and Jaipur, State Bank of Hyderabad. State Bank of Jaipur and State Bank of Bikaner, which were two separate subsidiaries were merged into one in 1963 in to State Bank of Jaipur and Bikaner. This associated bank too has been merged into State Bank of India. Lately State Bank of India bailed out private sector Yes Bank by injecting equity.

AVIATION BROUGHT UNDER STATE CONTROL

The government came out with Air Corporations Act that nationalized the air transportation industry as well in the 1950s. Air

India started by Tatas in 1933 was nationalized with government of India purchasing majority stake in the carrier in August 1953 and it was made into Air India International Limited. All the airlines operating domestic services were transferred to a new company called Indian Airlines. With the Government coming out with new aviation policy after economic reforms to open up the Indian skies to private airlines, the two airlines were merged to form Air India. Now, Indian aviation industry is open to foreign direct investment as well. Air India, which had gone through turbulent times, is still among the top airlines in the country. But due to heavy losses suffered by it in recent years, government is vigorously pursuing its privatisation. In fact the lock down in recent months due to coronavirus pandemic has delayed its privatisation process. There are already several private airlines operating in India and Air India's share in domestic operation has been gradually slipping. It however continued to dominate in international operations that perhaps is one of the small attractions for private and foreign players to look at its acquisition.

Central warehousing Corporation, Export Credit Guarantee Corporation, Hindustan Photo Films, Hindustan Salts Ltd, ONGC and Neyveli Lignite Corporation were among those major public sector undertakings set up during the Second Five Year Plan. Some of them are leading public enterprises even today with maharatna and navratna status. Many of them are listed companies as well. One or two like Hindustan Photo films have become sick and has been hived off in the face of changing technology and digital photography. One unit of it is still making X-ray films.

Apart from expanding existing private and State-owned steel plants at Jamshedpur, Kulti-Burnpur, and Bhadravati, three new iron and steel plants were located at Bhilai, Durgapur, and Raurkela. Though Steel Authority of India has expanded its steel manufacturing activity across the country in subsequent deades, several private players apart from Tata, which existed even at the time of independence, have set up large steel plants in the country. It included Jindals, Arcelor Mittal apart from Tatas. South Korean steel major which wanted to set up a plant in Odisha, however has not taken off. India has one of the largest iron ore reserves in the World.

The Chittranjan Locomotive Workshop, the Hindustan Shipbuilding Yard (Vishakhapatnam), the Sindri Fertiliser Factory, and Hindustan Machine Tools Ltd. (HMT) at Bangalore were expanded during the second plan period. Hindustan Machine Tools, which expanded into several areas from watches to tactors to machine tools have since become a sick company and hived off some of the units.

There were some cost and time over-run in public sector projects due to non availability of timely finance and impediments in acquiring technology. Nevertheless these industries were set up in the country unleashing a new era of industrial development by creating much needed industrial base. The Second Five Year Plan described as Industrial and Transport Plan resulted in National Income increasing substantially. It however did not achieve the average annual growth of five per cent during the plan period. However Public Sector spread its tentacles in various parts of the country and in various sectors. By 1960 Public Sector was into Steel making, Fertilizer, Lignite mining and Power generation, Ship building, Heavy industries, Machine tools, Telephones, Civil Aviation, Railway coaches, engines, wagons, Photo films and many more areas. Significantly they were not concentrated in one area and had spread all over the country, including several backward areas. This also helped in development of many townships and new industrial growth centres in the country.

As the country moved into the 1960s, the public sector enterprises were well entrenched and spread its tentacles to new areas.

1956 Industrial Policy Resolution

1956 Industrial Policy Resolution was formulated to ensure that the state would endeavour in a manner that the ownership and control of the material resources of the country are distributed in a manner to serve the common good of the people. To ensure the 1956 policy provided direct responsibility to the Government for the development of industries in various parts of the country and in wide ranging areas.

Accordingly the policy resolution had two schedules A and B.

Schedule A listed 17 industries, which would be exclusive responsibility of the State to develop.

Schedule B contained 12 industries, which will be progressively State-owned. But private enterprises will supplement the efforts of the state in these industries.

Schedule A: The development of the following industries will be exclusive state responsibility:

- Arms and ammunition and allied defence equipment
- Atomic Energy
- Railways
- Air transport
- Power generation and distribution\
- Iron and Steel
- Aircraft manufacture
- Shipbuilding
- Coal and Lignite
- Telephone and Telephone cable, telegraph and wireless apparatus
- Mineral oils
- Heavy castings and forgings of iron and steel
- Plant and machinery for Iron and Steel, mining, machine tools and basic industries
- Heavy electrical plants including hydraulic steam turbines
- Mining or iron ore, manganese, chrorme, gypsum, sulphur gold and diamond
- Mining and procession of Copper, Lead, Zinc, Tin, Molybdenum and Worfram
- Minerals required for Atomic energy

Schedule B of industries where State would progressively own them and private sector is allowed to supplement government in these areas:

- All other minerals excepting minor minerals
- Aluminum and other non-ferrous metals
- Machine tools
- Ferro-alloys and tool steels
- Basic and intermediate products for chemical industries like drugs, dyestuffs and plastics
- Antibiotics and other essential drugs

- Fertilisers
- Synthetic rubber
- Carbonisation of coal
- Chemical pulp
- Road transport
- Sea transport

All the other industrial activities were left to private sector. But State had the option to enter in those areas as well if it felt the need.

CHAPTER 3

Indira Gandhi Committed to Taking Public Enterprises to Commanding Heights

Late Indira Gandhi, soon after taking over as Prime Minister in 1966 in difficult times declared: "we advocate Public Sector for three reasons: to gain control, to promote critical development in terms of social gain or strategic value rather than primarily as considerations of profit and to provide commercial surpluses with which to finance further economic development."

She was committed to pursuing vigorously the policy of strengthening public enterprises as PSUs took firm root in 1960s after two five year plans. It had got into basic and heavy industries. Nationalisation of insurance sector in the 1950s provided government some financial muscle to make Public enterprises get into critical areas for overall development of the country including agriculture.

National Seeds Corporation was among the first public sector enterprises to be set up in the early 1960s. Though a small company set up in 1963, it immensely helped in stepping up production of quality and certified seeds in the country. It contributed to the success of green revolution in the country that happened in the 1960s ensuring that India became self sufficient in food grains in subsequent years. Public sector enterprises like NSC and Food Corporation of India, also set up in mid 1960s, contributed to farm reform and moving towards food security of the country. India, which used to go with a begging bowl to import food grains, sometimes in the form of aid subsequently became foodgrain surplus and exporting country. Thanks to the vision of our leaders and the role of government and public enterprises. In this contribution of late Lal Bahadur Shastri, who was prime minister for a short period, late C Subramaniam as food and agriculture minister then, agro scientist Dr M S Swaminathan, were invaluable.

The two wars with China and Pakistan in1962 and 1965 however slowed the pace of public sector development as resources had to be diverted to fighting the wars and buying weapons from abroad as India did not have many enterprises manufacturing defence equipment at that time. But a spin off of the wars was hastening of manufacturing of defence equipment in the public sector. Ordnance factories were set up, which were directly under the supervision of Defence Ministry. Hindustan Aeronautics was set up in Bangalore in 1964 and Battle tank factory at Avadi near Chennai. An Ordnance factory was set up to manufacture army trucks at Jabalpur. More Hal factories were set up in Kanpur and Nashik. Several other factories for manufacture of defence equipment also came up. The Third Five Year Plan had an ambitious road map to build on the foundation laid by the Second Plan but resource crunch slowed down the process a bit and the momentum picked up subsequently. Companies like BHEL expanded to set up more units in various parts of the country. Steel, critical input for defence equipment, infrastructure and housing too got a boost with more steel plants being set up in the 1960s

India faced severe drought for two consecutive years resulting in renewed thrust to agriculture development, which brought about green revolution in the country. This too had a spin-off effect in the development of State owned companies both at the Centre and the States. Food Corporation of India, one of the largest PSEs in the country was set up at that point of time in 1966 with the objective of ensuring remunerative prices to farmers through procurement at minimum support price. It also ensured that public distribution was put in place so that common man got food grains in the entire country through a network of fair price shops. Other warehousing corporations came up in central and state sectors. Tele-communications sector expanded. Railways set up some manufacturing units. Integral coach Factory was set up in Chennai and several wagon manufacturing units were set up in Eastern and other parts of the country. Chittaranjan Locomotives for manufacture of electric engines in West Bengal and Diesel Locomotives for manufacture of diesel engines at Varanasi were set up.

In fact the strategy provided by the Second Five Year Plan to develop public sector to a commanding height was pursued not only in Third Five Year Plan but also subsequent two five year plans.

Although the first half of the decade 1960-70 was hindered due to external factors, the pivotal role of the public sector as an instrument of socio-economic development was not lost sight of. The impediments including severe drought situation did not deter government to build upon the foundation laid in the 1950s so that industrialization process was pursued with the stress on basic and heavy industries. There was no let up in moving towards building infrastructure, reducing inequalities, job creation, balanced regional development, minimizing outflow of foreign exchange and moving on to producing those goods and services which were in short supply. As a result the public sector during this period achieved dominant position in the country in the manufacture of steel, fuel and power, machine-building and chemical industries. These industries were fundamental to rapid economic growth and determine the pace at which the economy can become self-reliant and self-generating. These PSEs in the 1960s helped in developing defence production, housing and other infrastructure.

BANK NATIONALISATION

The decade also saw public sector get a foot hold into the services sector. It entered engineering consultancy, expanded into insurance and banking, particularly after the nationalization of 14 major private banks in 1969. More banks were nationalized in the next decade to take the number of public sector banks to 27. Lately mergers in public sector banks have brought down to 10 Psu banks of which six are large ones in the face of mergers of big ones. The merger process is yet to be fully completed.

NON-LIFE INSURANCE NATIONALISATION FOLLOWED

Following bank nationalization non-life insurance was nationalized in the early part of 1970s. Earlier in 1950s, Life Insurance came under government umbrella with the formation of LIC. This gave government more financial muscle to carry out government plans. Also with insurance and banking in Public Sector, government's financial muscle for more investments in PSEs and for social sector projects improved considerably. Government also earned by way of dividends from Public Sector contributing to the financial health of the centre and states.

These steps were necessary to creating large surpluses for development so as to improve rate of economic growth. Simultaneously the Third Plan continued with the government efforts to build small industries as a vital segment in the industrial structure. This helped in not only integrating large and small industries but ensure that Industrialization percolated to the rural areas. It brought about modernization of traditional industries in rural areas.

During the third Five Year Plan a debate emerged on whether government should prioritise industrial or agricultural development. But Government felt it was not either or but that there has to be balanced growth between the two. Questions were raised by captains of industry on why government should produce more and more steel. To this the government then explained that steel is one commodity for which there is always need in the economy. The more one produced the more it will get absorbed as the per capita consumption of steel is one of the lowest in the world even today.

Prime Minister Jawaharlal Nehru said during the debate in Parliament on the Draft Third Five Year Plan that "it does not matter how much steel you produce—three times, ten times, fifty times—you will always find a use for it. It does not matter how much power you produce, you will always find a use for it in India with her growing economy. To say, that we may not find use for the steel that we shall produce is to look at things in a most restricted and limited way, not realizing the dynamics of social growth."

So the Third Five-Year Plan was formulated in this background to achieve a self-generating and self-reliant economy by 1975-76. It planned to achieve 5 per cent average growth with self sufficiency in food grain production and expand basic industries. It also made provision for expanding growing demand of population for food grains, cloth, steel, power, coal, transport and jobs, education and skill development.

To achieve this, the outlay for public sector was stepped up to Rs 7,500 crore. But lot of frustration came in the way of implementing the Third Plan because of Sino-Indian war in 1962, Indo-Pak war in 1965 and severe drought in 1966. The period saw industrial recession and high inflation and foreign exchange crisis as well resulting in devaluation of rupee in 1966. Government converted these challenges into opportunity and put in place necessary public institutions that led to putting the economy back on rails. This ensured that the path of planned development with public sector occupying pride of place took deep roots in the economy. Of course, Government had to resort to plan holiday for three years, which were replaced by annual plans for three consecutive years from 1966-69, before the Fourth Five Year Plan was formulated to fulfill the objectives that was enunciated in the 1956 Industrial Policy Resolution. The annual plans were basically meant to complete the unfulfilled projects particularly in the public sector during the Third Plan. Due to hiccups the Third Five Year Plan ending in 1966 could average a mere 2.5 per cent growth against the 5 per cent target. As public enterprises formed the backbone of planned development, there were delays and hiccups in PSU growth too.

Some far-reaching developments took place during the 1960s that improved financial muscle of the country. These ensured much needed resources were found for both agriculture and industrial development. After the Chinese aggression, the defence allocation was raised from Rs 300 crore to 1000 core, diverting money from development expenditure mainly from the allocation for public sector development.

The Government perceived new and innovative steps to mobilize savings from public for development. One of the criticisms of the Mahalanobis growth model in the Second Plan, was that it did not pay adequate attention to mobilizing savings while promoting investment in Heavy Industries in the Public Sector. These industries have long gestation period and until they become self-generating, resources had to be found from other sources.

To find the much needed resources for Third Five Year Plan investment in public sector and defence production, Government set up Unit Trust of India in 1964 on the lines of Unit Trust of Britain and mutual funds in United States through an Act of Parliament. The purpose of setting up UTI was aimed at mobilizing savings from small and middle income groups. The money garnered was invested in financial instruments. These instruments could be resold providing liquidity. Another imaginative development in 1964 was setting up of Industrial Development Bank of India to accelerate industrial growth by providing long term funds. This was based on the model of Industrial Development Bank of Japan. Development banks are necessary to tap public money through bonds for long-term investments in infrastructure projects. The closure of development banks in the first decade of 2000 is partly responsible for the present banking crisis. The commercial banks, which get short to medium term funds have been forced to lend long term resulting in asset-liability mismatch. Commercial banks mobilise resources short to medium term by definition and lend short to medium terms. Long term lending is usually done by development banks are through corporate bonds.

FOOD CORPORATION OF INDIA

Food Corporation of India was formed in 1966 with green revolution taking roots particularly in Punjab and Haryana. With its wide network and massive godowns all over the country. It is among the leading public sector undertakings in the country. But lately there is a view emerging that the organisation has outlived its utility in an era of plenty of food grains and liberalization and the need to restructure it.

The government got into warehousing business much before setting up of FCI with Central warehousing corporation in 1957. CWC got into all commodities and FCI was meant primarily for food grains procurement and maintain stocks including buffer for public distribution system.

After a plan holiday of three years, in the face of economy having been shattered due to two wars with China and Pakistan in 1962 and 1965 and two years of severe drought in the mid 1960s, the government got back to planned development and fourth five plan was formulated in 1969, the year in which 14 top private banks were nationalised to mobilise much needed resources for pro-poor policies and public sector development.

Fourth Plan too vigorously pursued self-reliance and accelerated the progress towards socialist society. It emphasised on development of public sector, besides reducing dependence on foreign aid. It made all out efforts to utilise fully existing capacity so that unnecessary investments were not made in areas where there was excess capacity. It laid emphasis on growth of industries like machinery, chemicals, mines, power and transport, which helped in bringing about self-reliance. The total outlay of the plan was Rs 24,398 crore, of which public sector was provided Rs 14,398 crore investment. The industry, mainly transport, power and mining were provided 26.5 per cent of outlay. Even in agriculture the Fourth Plan concentrated in development of farm inputs like irrigation, water and pump sets, fertilizers, improved varieties of seeds. Public sector had a critical role to play. The Plan also provided adequate expansion in the supply of consumer goods, while expending the basic and heavy industries.

To bring about price stability, the plan pushed public sector to get into areas, which would help increase the supply of essential consumer goods like cloth, vegetable oil, soap, cement, sugar, drugs and so on. Private sector was already there in these areas and they were also encouraged to step up production.

As more public sector enterprises came into being, their functioning came into scrutiny. It was realised as in rest of the World that social purpose cannot be adequately achieved unless the functioning of the organisation as an enterprise is successful and generates adequate returns for the investments. Experts felt there was need for giving greater attention to the successful functioning of public sector enterprises.

The issues like more autonomy to the management of public sector, quality of entrepreneurship, appointment of technocrats to head of public sector enterprises instead of appointing IAS officers and other bureaucrats surfaced in the late 1960s. But these criticisms were not widespread as in the late 1970s and in 1980s, which subsequently led to liberalisation of the economy in 1991.

But in 20 years since independence, Public Sector had achieved great deal in terms of their contribution to quantitative targets of production, to the establishment of a modern industrial structure, to balanced regional development and to the formation of technological skills. Public sector also became principal instruments of planning in India, occupying commanding heights of the economy, controlling and directing in a large measure the whole course of development. Apart from industrial transformation, it contributed to the rapid development of key sectors like trade, banking and insurance, transport, shipping, aviation, steel, power and so on.

In countries like South Korea, Taiwan and Japan, there was a debate in the post-war period on whether public sector should be encouraged in poor and developing economy for the development of infrastructure and other basic industries. They were of the view that in the short-term it may be worthwhile following this approach but in the long term private sector would have to eventually emerge as dominant sector.

But India's founding fathers at that time did not subscribe to this view and felt that in view of the complexities of the domestic situation in a vast country like India, socialistic approach will help in eradicating mass poverty in fastest possible time. This will also prevent concentration of economic power and wealth in private hands. Where there are technological considerations, public control was preferred. Fourth plan document released in July 1970 clearly reiterated government's position as socialism involves reordering of society on rational and equitable basis and it can be achieved only by assigning an expanding role to the public sector. In order to achieve self-reliance and strong economic foundation, the approach at that time rejected idea of determining inter-sectoral allocation primarily by market forces in some of the under-developed economies.

BUREAU OF PUBLIC ENTERPRISES

With public sector growing in strength, in early 1960s, Bureau of Public Enterprises, conceived by the then Steel and Finance Minister T T Krishnamachari to oversee the working of result oriented managers of public sector. It also helped in tackling wage issues and industrial relations in public enterprises. Of course this organisation was wound up 25 years later after severe criticism of this organisation as yet another power centre.

FIRST ATTEMPT TO EVALUATE PERFORMANCE OF PSUs AFTER 2 DECADES

On the basis of the experience gained on the performance of public sector undertakings for nearly two decades, government made its first attempt to evaluate their management. In the 1950s and 1960s, civil servants were mostly drawn into managing the affairs of PSUs. Appointments to top PSU posts were made directly by the concerned administrative ministry. Most of them came from administrative services, the technical services like the Railways, Public Works Department and Army Engineering Services.

In 1958-59, for the first time an industrial management pool was constituted for appointment of professional managers in PSUs.

In 1965, a major policy reform was brought about in selection procedures by constituting a screening committee of secretaries to assess the suitability of persons applying for PSU posts. This brought about some improvement in appointing competent professional. However this needed to be improved upon, in subsequent years hence The Public Enterprises Selection Board was set up in 1974 for appointment of top posts in PSUs. In 1969, a new order was effected wherein government officers serving in public sector in top positions had to opt within two or three years for career in the public sector or return to their parent cadre. (So that they did not have best of both the Worlds).

The public sector by now had received utmost attention from planners. The great push given to the public sector in the initial Five Year Plans have also helped in the development of human resource in backward areas for changing the traditional character of village life.

Many public sector undertakings have been set up in the backward areas to capitalise on the rural labour through vocational education, technical training and managerial skills. PSUs have and continued to take special interest in setting up community development centres to discharge their social responsibility. In the first three decades after independence PSUs covered almost all segments of the economy—agriculture, commerce, industry, finance and banking, research and development, public utilities, cultural and social affairs.

Indian Oil Corporation, which was set up in 1964 is even today among the star performers in the country. It is not only the largest corporate entity in both the public and private sectors, it is also among the few Indian companies in fortune 500 global companies. IOC was set up by amalgamating the Indian Refineries Ltd, having refineries at Nunmati in Assam and Barauni in Bihar and Indian Oil Company, which was incorporated earlier in 1959. IOC had two refineries at Guwahati and Baravni. Subsequently ONGC transferred its Gujarat Refinery to IOC in 1965. A Maharatna company has several refineries all over the country and has built a few more including one in Pradip in Odisha. At the moment It had refining capacity of around 60 million tonnes. ONGC, Neyveli Lignite Corporation, BHEL, which were set up in the 1950s, have grown substantially and they expanded their operations in the 1960s. ONGC and BHEL are among the Maharatna companies in the country. These companies have done well right from the beginning and their performance has only improved post liberalisation of the economy. Many of the Public Sector companies have become large conglomerates and have contributed to the nation building. Their performance is comparable with the best in private sector and some of them have done even better. There were some problems and hiccups as objectives of public enterprises kept changing with the time. Earlier the emphasis was to adopt labour intensive technology and lately its modern capital intensive technology and hence resulting at times in clash of objectives.

Hindustan Machine Tool, which was originally set up in 1953 to manufacture tractors and food processing machines, got into more areas like manufacture of watches, printing machines, precision machines including lathes and so on in the 1960s and these units were set up in new locations across the country. It is a different matter that ITI and HMT, which served industrialisation of the country in the 1950s to 1980s, outlived its utility as they did not change with time and modernise both management and manufacturing practices. One of the problems of HMT was it got into diversified manufacturing from watches, to tractors, to machine tools and so on. Because of unified cadre, at times watch expert was transferred to head tractor unit and the like resulting in poor management practices. This partly contributed to the poor management of the company, besides heavy overheads and obsolescence of technology. ITI was a monopolistic industry in the telecom sector where technology change very rapidly. Unfortunately ITI failed to recognise it and made no attempt to collaborate or do research and development to keep up with the changing technology. This led to its downfall.

With growing requirement of cotton, particularly by flourishing textile industry in the country, Public Sector got into this sector with the setting up of Cotton Corporation of India in July 1970 to act as canalising agency for import of cotton particularly for long and extra-long staple varieties. Subsequently the role of the corporation underwent several changes and currently its role is to ensure remunerative and competitive prices to the cotton farmers. India, which faced shortage of cotton, now is the second largest producer of cotton with the introduction of hybrid and genetically modified varieties. It produces over 35 million tonnes of the crop with sizeable exports of raw cotton every year. In the 1960s a public sector company was set up even to deal in metal scrap. A Metal Scrap Trading company was set up in 1964 based in Kolkata indicating how deep and widespread public sector went into so as to remove all obstacles in industrialisation through government intervention and participation. Even Handloom and Handicrafts exports, corporations were set up in late 1950s.

With private sector not responding adequately and effectively, public sector got into more and more areas to remove obstacles to economic development.

CHAPTER 4

Bangladesh War Strengthened Role of PSUs in 1970 in Critical Areas

The decade of 1970 began with refugee problem with influx of 10 million people from East Pakistan that led to an India-Pakistan war and liberation of Bangladesh. Nearly a quarter-century of industrialisation through development of Public sector helped India show its military prowess in the war with India made Gnat aircraft at Hindustan Aeronautics, India assembled Mig 21 Soviet made fighter aircraft, India made Vijayanta tanks, naval frigates and several other armaments. Also public sector organisation like Food Corporation of India and other warehousing corporations helped in ensuring adequate availability of food to feed the millions of refugees coming from across the border. The Green Revolution in which Public Sector National seeds Corporation too contributed apart from several public sector fertiliser companies including Fertiliser Corporation of India, National Fertilisers, Rashtriya Chemicals and Fertilisers, Hindustal Fertilisers, Madras Fertilisers. Several fertiliser companies belogning to state governments too played a role in green revolution that had made India world leaders in production of several agri products like Rice, Wheat, Milk, fruits, vegetables, cotton and so on. India is still deficient in oilseeds production.

TURBULENT 1970S

The early years of 1970s were turbulent. The refugee problem and the Indo-pak war were followed by global oil crisis of 1973 resulting in crisis situation in the economy. But the strong Industrial and agricultural base driven by public sector development coupled with

Bank Nationalisation in 1969, setting up of Unit Trust of India and Industrial Development Bank of India ensured that Indian economy was resilient enough to weather the storm. ONGC stepped up oil exploration particularly after global oil crisis following a Middle-East war that began in the late 1960s, bore fruits with discovery of large quantity of oil and gas in Bombay High in mid 1970s that came as a breather to the economy already hit by balance of payment crisis due to skyrocketing of oil prices. Here again public sector ONGC played a critical role. At one point of time experts believed the oil find in Bombay High could make India meet most of its requirement domestically. That was not to be as oil requirement grew at much faster pace with economic development and new finds of domestic oil eluding the country. Subsequently some large quantity of gas was found in Krishna-Godaveri Basin but that again is not yet fully exploited.

The approach to planned development in an under developed country is not merely to get better results within the existing framework of economic and social institutions, but to mould and refashion these so that they contribute effectively to the realisation of wider and deeper social values. This applied more so to Fourth and Fifth Five Year Plan, which started off well after several problems during Third Five Year Plan. The entire planning process virtually got derailed because of two wars and severe drought in the 1960s. Yet the country did not give up planning process and came back with a bang after three years of delay in implementing the Fourth Five Year Plan. The initial years of the Fourth Plan were good for Public sector development in the country though government faced a huge strain on resources. Public Sector companies established themselves in many spheres of activity by then as India celebrated 25 years of independence in 1972.

SAMPLE SURVEY SHOWED RAPID PSU GROWTH

A sample survey of ten manufacturing public sector undertakings showed that the average annual growth rate of PSUs were 78 per cent during 1970-80. Madras Refineries topped the list with an average annual growth rate of 214 per cent followed by BHEL 206 per cent and HMT 103 per cent. In trading MMTC recorded average annual growth of 121 per cent, followed by STC 70 per cent and FCI 43 per cent.

The survey also went into the performance of top ten multinational companies in India. It found the average annual growth of MNCs were just 22 per cent during 1970-80 with Larson and Toubro at the top at 35 per cent. The achievement of PSU was spectacular. The top MNCs growth was far behind in India at that time.

Prime Minister Indira Gandhi conducted the first ever India's nuclear explosion in 1974, which worsened the economic situation. The oil crisis put strains on government's resources and sanctions by advanced nations led by United States hit the economy severely delaying the launch of second stage of development to take on competition.

The sharp increase in prices of food, fertilizers and oil seriously upset the assumptions made with regard to Public Sector outlay in draft Fifth Five Year Plan which was to begin in 1974. There was a churning in Planning Commission as well. This led to Fifth five year plan size being reduced and large outlay for the Industry was severely pruned. There were arguments for and against cutting the plan size. But the economic situation improved, after new oil find in Bombay High by public sector ONGC in the mid 1970s. This helped in putting the economy back on rails and the Fifth Plan was able to provide top priority to public sector development once again. Labour unrest in Railways and sick textile units too slowed the development and created some difficulty. Sick private textiles mills were taken over by the government to preserve jobs. The mills became sick due to the failure to invest periodically in modernisation. A new state owned National Textiles corporation was formed to run more than 100 sick private mills taken over in various parts of the country in 1973.

After overcoming various economic hurdles growth process was revived through the implementation of fifth plan. With government getting back its confidence with ONGC striking oil, the plan proposed higher level of annual average GDP growth 5.5 per cent through higher investment, efficiency and savings. This meant more investment in public sector, which was stepped up to Rs 37,350 crore of the total plan outlay of Rs 53,411 crore. Public Sector, despite its shortcomings, remained engine of growth and in narrowing regional disparities. The emergency imposed by the then Prime Minister Indira Gandhi was certainly a blot on India's democracy but as far as public sector was concerned, it injected more discipline and efficiency due to the fear of stringent action against erring workers and officials. This made them more accountable and resulted in marked improvement in PSU performance.

With Janata Party, the first non-congress government, coming to power in 1977, the Fifth Plan was aborted and Sixth Five year Plan was formulated in 1978 that attempted to dilute the importance of public enterprises in nation building. But Congress came back to power in mid-term elections in 1980 and the new government decided to rework the sixth five year plan restoring its earlier strategy of development through public enterprises. So the sixth plan was implemented from 1980-1985. The average annual growth proposed at 4.7 per cent by Janata government was reworked to achieve higher 5.2 per cent growth by substantially increasing the outlay for public sector from Rs 69,300 crore to Rs 84,000 crore.

The finished steel production in India, one of the basic industries that indicate the level of economic development, had grown from a mere 1.1 million tonnes in 1951 to 29.27 million tonnes in 2000-2001. During the first two decades of planned economic development, i.e. 1950-60 and 1960-70, the average annual growth rate of steel production exceeded 8 per cent. However, this growth rate could not be maintained in the following decades. During 1970-80, the growth rate in steel production came down to 5.7 per cent per annum and picked up marginally to 6.4 per cent per annum during 1980-90, which increased to 6.65 per cent per annum during 1990-2000.

Per capita steel consumption is still low. But steel industry is still growing in India and it is likely to touch 110-120 million tonnes per annum by 2020. More than half of it came from Public Sector.

The period between 1951 and 1965 witnessed an increase in industrial production by 2.8 times, whereas the period 1966–80 saw an increase by only 1.8 times. On compound rate of growth it was 5.8 per cent for the three decades. The rates for the 1951–60, 1960– 70 and 1970–80 decades were: 6.9 per cent, 6.3 per cent, and 4.2 per cent respectively. For 1951–65 it was 7.7 per cent and for 1965–80, it was 4 per cent. The rate of growth was negative for the year 1966 and 1967 with 0.5 per cent and 0.4 per cent respectively. For all other years it was positive. The growth rates were marked by wide fluctuations. The emphasis on industrial policies remained more or less same during the three decades except during the two and a half years of Janata rule when they came out with a new Industrial Policy Resolution only to be reversed after congress led by Indira Gandhi came back to power in 1980.

The rate of Industrial growth had fallen short of targets, especially during the post-third plan period. For example, 4th and the 5th plans stipulated the rates of growth at 8 per cent, as against this, the rates realized were just 4.7 per cent and 5.9 per cent respectively.

The reason given by the Monopolies Inquiry Commission (MIC) for targets not being met was that the industrial licensing system enabled big business houses to obtain disproportionately large share of licenses which led to pre-emption and foreclosure of capacity.

Subsequently, the Industrial Licensing Policy Inquiry Committee (Dutt Committee) constituted in 1967, recommended that larger industrial houses should be given licenses only for setting up industry in core and heavy investment sectors, thereby necessitating reorientation of industrial licensing policy.

In 1969, the Monopolies and Restrictive Trade Practices (MRTP) Act was introduced to enable the government to effectively control concentration of economic power. The Dutt Committee had defined large business houses as those with assets of more than Rs. 350 million. The MRTP Act, 1969, defined large houses as those with assets of Rs. 200 million and above. Large industries were designated as MRTP companies and were eligible to participate in industries that were not reserved for the Government or the small scale sector.

The new Industrial Licensing Policy of 1970 classified industries into four categories. First category, termed as 'Core sector', consisted of basic, critical and strategic industries. Second category termed as 'Heavy Investment sector' comprised projects involving investment of more than Rs. 50 million. The third category, the 'Middle sector' consisted of projects with investment in the range of Rs. 10 million to Rs. 50 million. The fourth category was 'De-licensed sector' in which investment was less than Rs. 10 million and was exempted from licensing requirements. The industrial licensing policy of 1970 confined the role of large business houses and foreign companies to the core, heavy and export-oriented sectors. With a view to prevent excessive concentration of industrial activity in the large industrial houses, a new industrial policy statement was issued in 1973.

In the first 15-year period of planned economic development, the public sector is credited to have been instrumental in securing rapid import substituting industrialization. It also provided the much needed economic infrastructure for initiating a self-reliant growth process and perhaps macro-economic stabilization as well. Public Sector however might not have been cost-effective in these years.

The next 15 years, there was relative stagnation of industrial sector partly because of perceptible slow down of the growth of public investment because several external factors coupled with drought in certain years. The three wars and oil crisis contributed significantly to the slowdown.

But there were significant reforms in the public sector since 1980s that brought about dramatic turnaround and in subsequent years for public sector to grow rapidly.

Subsidies including hidden, is considered to be one of the major reasons by economists for low return on investment in public enterprises in the early stages of planning which was corrected to a great extent post economic reforms in 1991. One point that needed to be taken note of is that growth rate of manufacturing in private sector increased from 4.4 per cent per annum during 1960-61 to 6.5 per cent per annum in 1979-80. But manufacturing in public sector continued to grow at an unchanged rate of 6.6 per cent per annum during the entire period beginning 1960-61. This only proves the point about public sector contribution to the economic development. Many of the upheavals that happened during that time were unforeseen external factors.

Nationalisation of sick textile mills in 1973 to protect the interest of lakhs of workers too contributed to erosion of profitability of public sector undertakings. The National Textile Corporation Limited (NTC), a Central Public Sector Enterprises was formed in April 1968 for managing sick private textile mills taken over by the Government. Starting with 16 mills in 1968, this number gradually rose to 103 by 1972–73. In 1974, Sick Textile Undertakings (Nationalisation) Act was passed by Parliament. All sick units were nationalised and the number of such units increased to 119 by 1995. Now there are 23 working textile mills producing yarn and fabric and 77 have been closed down. NTC has modernised 18 mills and is in the process of setting up three composite mills. One of the reasons for sickness in these mills was that they were old, some of them more than a century at the time of nationalisation. No modernisation had taken place resulting in units not being able to compete with modern mills. The units became sick as the owners did not have the money to invest in one go.

Though PSUs have been attacked time and again for its inefficiently but its contribution to nation building cannot be overlooked. This has been corroborated by late Justice S Rangarajan who said as Chairman of the MRTP Commission, "I had occasions to deal with private sector and therefore my long distance look at the public sector and my more intimate look at the private sector, helps me to have a certain kind of understanding in a comparative framework. It is no longer true to say that public sector enterprises are not efficient and private sector enterprises are efficient, because it has proven that sick industries can be taken over and managed better in the public sector."

PSU DEVELOPMENT DURING JANATA ERA 1977-80

The Government led by Prime Minister Morarji Desai decided to provide new dimension to planning and reconstituted the Planning Commission with D T Lakadawala as Deputy Chairman. A renowned economist Lakadawala has done a lot of research on poverty.

The reconstituted planning commission came out with a new idea of annual rolling plan that would provide more flexibility within the five year perspective.

The sixth plan as proposed by Janata government drastically changed the earlier philosophy for promoting industrial development through vigorous effort to push public sector. Instead it decided to promote agriculture and rural development and related industries like fertilizer and irrigation, to increase farm productivity.

The new Industry policy statement of Janata government in 1977 aimed at removing certain distortions in the previous Industrial Policy Resolution. The statement said it was also an attempt to provide a closer interaction between the agriculture and industry. The government decided to accord highest priority to the power generation and transmission. It expanded the list of industries exclusively reserved for small scale sector to over 500 items from 180. The list was to be reviewed every year. Special legislation was brought in to protect small and cottage industries, Khadi and village industries were encouraged and 22 village industries were to be developed apart from setting up district industries centres.

The areas where large industries could be set up was limited to basic industries, essential for infrastructure and those vital for small and village industries like steel, non-ferrous metals, cement and oil refineries. It also allowed large industries in capital goods, high technology industries like petrochemicals, fertilizers and pesticides and those that were outside the industrial items reserved for small scale industries.

To promote Indian owned industries, it pushed foreign companies to reduce their foreign equity below 40 per cent as per the guidelines of Foreign Exchange Regulation Act of 1973 (FERA).

There were some exceptions to it like highly export oriented industries or companies with sophisticated technology. Two multinational companies which refused to comply with the FERA regulation Coca Cola and IBM were forced to shut down their operations. The two companies came back to India after economic reforms of 1991. FERA was considered draconian and was later diluted and new Foreign Exchange Management Act (FEMA) came into being.

Janata Government decided not to give licenses for setting up industries within certain limits of large cities in the country.

With political turmoil during the period not many industries came up barring those which were in the pipeline. The growth of Public Sector was dismal during the period and Industrial Policy and Sixth Five Year Plan reworked after congress came back to power in 1980.

A new Industrial Policy Resolution was announced in 1980 by the then Prime Minister Indira Gandhi, was based on the 1956 Industrial Policy Resolution. While it returned to the previous policy of taking Public Sector back to commanding heights, it decided on some stock taking of performance of PSUs.

Considering the general loss of people's faith on PSU, the government decided to take corrective steps to improve efficiency of PSUs, review the management and come out with solutions like providing more autonomy, professionalization of management and running some of the units on commercial lines.

There were inense discussion on public sector enterprises in Parliament periodically. The autonomy and accountability came up for discussion particularly when reports of committee on public undertakings were tabled. Time and again it was pointed out that full ministerial responsibility and bureaucratic administration is inconsistent with a commercial type organisation, and autonomous public enterprises would have to be treated differently than the departments of the government, if they have to produce results.

According to professor Laxmi Narain of Osmania University as early as 1948, when first industrial policy resolution was formulated, the central government had decided to run public enterprises differently. Autonomous enterprises were thus accepted as an essential and inevitable part of the system. But in practice, Parliament and the government had hardly respected autonomous status of public enterprises and there were several examples in this regard. Parliament's lack of appreciation for the autonomy of public corporations has been summed up by H Venkatasubbiah in his book Indian Economy since Independence. Professon A H Hanson and Paul Appleby, an U S expert, too have felt that Parliament members were not in favour of autonomy even though the top leaders always supported the principle of autonomy. There was a growing feeling particularly after 1977, the overbearing approach of the parliamentary committees on Public enterprises particularly with regard to spending on infructuous expenditure, publicity and advertising. This was at a time when Public sector undertakings profit had soared to Rs476 crore in 1976-77, an improvement of 64 per cent over the previous year as per Bureau of Public Enterprises figure. This overbearing approach was temporary as government changed in 1980 and government reverted to earlier policy of not being overbearing on public enterprise managers.

In the real life situation, there was always compromise of autonomy, be it in purchase of indigenous machinery, appointment of directors wage negotiations, day to day functioning and so on. A thinking also emerged on hybrid management to inject more autonomy by diluting government stake to 51 per cent. There was a suggestion that 49 per cent ownership may be delegated the task of running these units in their own way within the overall policy guidelines of 51 per cent government stake, and leave the issues settled by the forces of professional management decisions on the boards of these companies.

As the decade closed there were also thinking in some of the countries about privatisation of public sector undertakings, particularly in United Kingdom and France. In 1979, China decided to move away from totally communist country where the state owned everything. Chinese economy opened up under Deng Xiao Ping, private and foreign investments were allowed gradually, which led to nearly three decades of double-digit growth making the economy second largest in the World, next only to United States. All over the World, after the second World War ll, there was a trend towards socialistic pattern of development where public sector played a critical role. Over 3-4 decades after the war and depression many countries in Europe and Asia were in reconstruction and redevelopment mode after devastation and economic collapse and state had to play crucial role as private individuals were not forthcoming.

After four decades, stock taking of public enterprises world over began to fix some of the ills that came with excessive control. India was no exception.

CHAPTER 5

Public Sector Grows in Strength in 1980s in India; Elsewhere its Privatisation Begins

As disinvestment and privatisation began in 1980s in advanced economies spearheaded by British Prime Minister Margret Thatcher, India continued its faith on public enterprises, perhaps rightly so as the economy had not yet started the reform process for private sector take off on the back of the foundation laid by the public enterprise in India.

Late Rajiv Gandhi, soon after he assumed as Prime Minister in 1984 end voiced his commitment to promoting public enterprises even as he attempted to stitch a framework for liberalisation of the economy. With communist China beginning the opening up process in 1979 under Deng Xiaoping, some experts started some debating half heartedly on whether India should open up or not.

At a round table of India organized by the European Management Foundation in April 1985, Rajiv Gandhi made it clear in no uncertain terms about his support to public enterprises. "... The public sector is the core of India's industrial development and we use it as a tool for opening up backward and non industrial areas to industry and to development.... The development role of our public sector has been very critical in the development of India. And we must keep this in mind when we criticize public sector enterprises for their inefficiency or their lower productivity, because we forced them to go into areas where there is no industry, where there is no infrastructure, may be no roads, no communications, no facilities."

BY 1980S PSU BECOME A MAJOR SOURCE OF WEALTH CREATION

By early 1980s, Public Sector in India had become a major source of wealth creation growing with market confidence besides boosting self-reliance in the country. Also the public enterprises had perhaps entered many of the key sectors contribiting greatly to sustainable economic development. Though the sector faced several road blocks, the growth was steady and acted as a catalyst for both private sector, small scale industries and social sectors. The march of public sector was unstoppable with the capital employed in Central public sector undertakings at Rs 32,203 crore and total turnover of Rs 46,777 crore by 1983-84. From a mere five enterprises in 1951, it had grown to 209 in 1983 employing more than two million people. PSU units got into light manufacturing, consumer goods, electronics, high-tech products, construction, consultancy services and even tourism and hotel industries.

DEMAND FOR PRIVATISATION OF PSUS IN INDIA

With growing demand for privatisation of public sector enterprises in advanced economies in the late 1970s and early 1980s to improve efficiency, there was an attempt in India too. There were some efforts to lay more emphasis on development of small scale enterprises in the late 1970s and accordingly the Industrial Policy was tweaked by Janata Government in 1977. But this was reversed with the Congress government coming back to power in 1980

The July 1980 Industrial policy statement therefore shifted the emphasis on PSUs to optimising utilization of installed capacity, maximizing production and productivity, job creation, reducing regional imbalance, promotion of export oriented industries and set up those industries that would help in checking rising prices and quality to ensure consumer protection. Public Enterprises too were emerging strong in many sectors as they took on internal and external competition. This made the government to explore the possibilities of public enteprises entering into consumer industries as a price stability measure and to ensure improved availability.

This follows recommendation of Parliamentary Committee on Public Undertakings (COPU) in 1980-81 in this regard. COPU's 49th report said the Government's objective should be to expand public sector into new fields including production of mass consumption goods in areas where significant production gaps existed like tyre and tube industry, where foreign companies dominated and shortage persisted.

The thinking at that time was that Public sector should progressively enter particularly in mass consumption items dominated by foreign companies so that it acts as a catalyst to set high examples to others and provide an effective means of regulating prices to protect the interest of the common man.

COPU therefore asked government to undertake a comprehensive study to identify areas of consumer industries.

The sectors like steel making , shipbuilding, heavy industries, machine tools, telephone equipment, aircraft manufacture, electronics, trucks and tanks for defence, railway engines, coaches, wagons, specialized steel, power equipment, generators, transformers, fertilizer, chemicals, drugs, oil exploration, crude oil production, oil refining did not face such problems as they were dominated by public sector. Also Public enterprises dotted all over the country providing opportunity for pursuing balanced development. This also ensured getting into consumer goods manufacture would not be a problem.

COPU stressed the need for a 'White paper' on PSUs periodically as is the practice in United Kingdom to take stock of PSU performance. Armed with COPU recommendation, Government announced in 1987 that it would bring out White Paper on PSUs. But somehow this was never implemented. However, Standing Conference on Public Enterprises brought out an approach Paper to the white Paper on Public Enterprises in December 1989 and later a Blueprint of SCOPE's White Paper on the Public Sector in April 1990. This Blueprint went into various aspects of Public enterprises like autonomy, corporate governance, corporate social responsibility, wage structure, commercial aspects, profitability, efficiency, technology, pricing, and labour and various other constraints and advantages.

The efforts to improve the overall net rate of return in the 1980s had mixed results. In fact the net profit of PSUs declined at that time and as a consequence Public enterprises could not generate adequate resources internally for new PSU investment proposals to take off. This is because basic industries output like that of steel, cement, fertiliser and textiles fell short of the target. But Seventh Plan as a whole in the mid-eighties did well in containing external debt and promoting Self reliance. This helped to marginally improve macro-economic fundamentals then.

Fiscal conservatism in the early stages of development and fiscal prudence in most of the other periods had ensured that India was financially stable despite being a poor country but later part of the 1980s saw India's debt management going awry as the government indulged in fiscal profligacy. Of Rs 3,22,366 crore outlay in the Seventh Five year Plan, public sector outlay was Rs 1,80,000 crore. Though the amount was huge in absolute terms, the public sector outlay had been reduced to 58 per cent of the plan outlay and private corporate sector accounted for 17 per cent of the outlay. This is because government was keen to tone up Public sector performance and subject to competition by encouraging private sector.

Economists and political leadership at that time felt it was time for making public sector units more efficient and financially viable. With the government budgets being heavily burdened with demands for development expenditure, government felt it was no longer in a position to make up for large deficiencies in public sector resources generation.

The government also came up with idea of entering into memorandum of understanding with PSUs. This also ensured higher measure of autonomy to public enterprises management. So PSUs gradually entering into MoUs but this gained ground only after economic reforms in 1991 with several of them including public sector banks signing MoUs. MoUs bound PSUs to achieve certain production and profit targets every year.

Several PSU chairmen and managing directors were also asked to come out with suggestions based on their experience. Most of them came to the conclusion that there was plenty of scope for improving the functioning of public sector undertakings. To achieve this they felt that public sector should be provided more autonomy to curtail the stranglehold of administrative ministries on them. They felt frequent changes in direction with the change in minister, government or bureaucrat needed to be curbed. They felt there was need to bring about attitudinal change towards public sector. Labour issues too cropped up with public sector employing huge number of people, particularly in sick industries taken over by the government. Failure to set up a managerial cadre for PSUs was one of the factors for poor management. There was national pride in serving the nation. But this gradually changed with younger generation taking over reins, and the national pride fading, the attitude changed.

The stock taking of PSU performance was not peculiar only to India at that time. It was happening in many parts of the World as Public enterprises set up in the post second world war era to promote socialistic and welfare pattern of development with several variations came increasingly under public scrutiny with their efficiency and profitability dipping with growing trade unionism and redundant labour due to increasing modernisation and automation of production processes. Countries like Britain and France were in the fore front as the reassessment of Public enterprises performance began at the fag end of the 1970s. Privatisation of public enterprises began in Britain and experience was mixed as it succeeded in some sectors like civil aviation and telecom but failed miserably in case of Railways. The experience showed blanket privatisation was not panacea for all ills of public enterprises. It had to be calibrated and done on a case by case basis.

In India too there was vigorous debate in 1980s on how to improve the functioning of public enterprises. One issue that became loud and clear was to provide greater autonomy to inject professionalism. Public enterprises role became more distinct, entrepreneurial skills were found to be lacking.

A view emerged that government should restrict itself to issuing policy directives, and the day-to-day functioning should be left to the management of public enterprises. The experts felt that powers and authority of public enterprises and the respective administrative ministries should be clearly defined. Overlapping powers should be phased out and oral instructions from the government should be avoided.

Public sector performance gradually came under public scrutiny and committees were set up to tone up the functioning. The morale in some of the PSUs was low because of the helplessness and inability of the top management to ask the government to implement even its own instructions.

Arjun Sen Gupta, Mohammed Fazal and L.K. Jha Committees were set up in the 1980s and they came out with some far reaching recommendations. Some of them were implemented in subsequent decades. COPU also came out with reports on management, and control, accountability and autonomy. Suggestions of these committees formed the basis for improving the functioning of public enterprises in the later part of 1980s. Some of the recommendations were implemented after economic reforms began in 1991. These were essential to take head on the challenges that came with the opening up of the economy. This became necessary with multinationals entering the market. In fact some of the public enterprises have done well and opening up of the economy had helped them to compete due to empowerment. Some even fared better than Private sector and transnational companies. There were some laggards as well, mostly those which could change with the time and modernise, improve efficiency, cut costs to take on competition. There were examples of inefficient companies falling by the way side in private sector as well. Hindustan Motors, manufacture of Ambassador car was a good example as it could not face the competition from Maruti Udyog, which was buy the way a joint venture with the central government at that point of time.

Concerned over the growing tendency of ministries to interfere in the working of the enterprises, the committees desired that necessary ground rules should be laid down to prevent government, transgressing into the spheres of detailed administration of PSUs. To ensure accountability, they wanted all instructions from the government to PSUs should be in writing. They also wanted more financial powers to PSUs.

Arjun Sen Gupta report in 1986 suggested measures to change the whole environment of operation of public enterprises. It also felt the modalities of instructions practiced in PSUs might have been appropriate when the number of enterprises were small and pioneering in nature. Now with changed situation and so many enterprises, some of them very large and diverse, required different approach.

It came out with detailed suggestions on providing more autonomy to PSUs, pricing of products, setting up of holding company for large PSUs, performance evaluation, wage policy for PSUs, productivity and technology upgradation and so on.

In 1983-84, L.K. Jha went into administrative reforms of government and public enterprises. The Jha committee came out with separate reports on public sector accountability, autonomy, administration, priced preference. It wanted PSU boards to be made professional and wanted government nominees in the board to be more active.

L.K. Jha, committee recommended that if the viability of public enterprises is to be ensured, decision making will have to be decentralised and the units must be given freedom to initiate, innovate and take risks, but be made accountable rather than having to comply with government rules all the time. This was considered to be drastic in an era socialism. Such a far-reaching course correction required political courage.

Some liberalisation process began during the 1980s. The most significant one at that time was delicensing of some of the industries. In 1985, 25 industries were delicensed and 20 more the very next year. In 1988, industries below Rs 15 crore investments were exempted from licensing. This cap was raised to Rs 50 crore if set up in backward areas. This facility was not available to FERA and MRTP companies.

Many Institutions including market regulator Securities and Exchange Board of India were set up. Credit Ratings Information Services of India and Over-the-Counter Exchange of India too were set up during the period. Steps were taken to remove price and distribution control apart from strengthening regulation.

The Seventh five year plan recognized the need to consolidate and enable the Indian industry to meet the emerging challenges. So a number of policy and procedural changes were brought about to increase productivity, reduce costs and improve quality. This helped India come out of the Hindu rate of economic growth that is below 3.5 per cent annual average growth. The economic growth was pushed up above 5 per cent in the 1980s, and further to 5-6 Percent later part of 1980s.

The government made attempts to free Public sector from a number of constraints so as to give more autonomy. But they were gradual and not drastic and disruptive. These steps helped in pushing industrial growth to an average 8.5 per cent during the Seventh Plan period. The endeavour of the Seventh Plan was to build a new India free from fear of want, exploitation. Five year plans with 15 years perspective was proposed by the then Deputy Chairman of Planning Commission Dr Manmohan Singh to take India to a new high and a confident economy in th 21st century.

Economists in general felt that the need of the hour was to progressively improve efficiency of public enterprises so as to attain global competitiveness in major products. Therefore the aim should be to make the country a modern, technologically progressive economy with expanding capacity to provide basic material and cultural requisites of well being for all people.

The Seventh Plan therefore adopted a strategy to upgrade technology of existing undertakings, reduce the cost of production and introduce new products. Special efforts were made to accelerate development in selected industries. The plan focused on bringing about energy security by stepping up power generation, oil exploration and production, increase production of coal and lignite and decided to pursue R&D effort on renewable energy like biomass, solar and wind.

Autonomy motivated managers to perform better. There was a growing view among experts at that time that Public sector managers were made accountable for results, but given no incentives to perform. They were often provided non-commercial goals, which were in conflict with profit maximization. For example capital intensive public enterprises had very limited scope for generating employment yet they were asked to fulfill the obligation of job creation. Political bosses also believed in keeping the objectives ambivalent. There is no standardization of relationship between public enterprises and government. Public enterprises affairs are often criticized in Parliament without giving opportunity for state enterprises to defend themselves. There was no professionalisation of management of public enterprises and decisions on growth, profitability and diversification were not taken on just business considerations.

Unlike in many of the European economies, fortunately in India there was no strong demand for privatisation of the public enterprises and in fact all political parties emphasised the strategic role of the Psus in development. But at the same time a stage had been reached in the late 1980s where unless the resource-generation capability of public enterprises improves substantially, the development process will be under jeopardy.

There was craving for more accountability and lavish spending in Public Sector came under scrutiny. The abuse of government owned five star hotels by directors and top bureaucrats came under public scrutiny. There was a time when Indian dignitaries used to get offended if entertained in company guest houses when five star ITDC hotels were available in that area.

R. C. Dutt, former Chairman and Managing Director of National Coal Development Corporation, while writing on the experience of Public Sector from 1950s to 1980s recalls how certain lavish behavior in public sector got institutionalised.

He said a common practice in Air India those days was to invite dignitaries to the inaugural flights and treat them lavishly. This not only resulted in spending scarce foreign exchange on such occasions but it also set an unhealthy pattern of lavish lifestyle.

Dutt recalled an interesting reaction of a minister during Indira Gandhi's government. Mohan Kumaramangalam, who was then director of Air India, was sent an invitation for a inaugural flight to United Kingdom among other countries. Kumaramangalam wrote back angrily to Air India declining the invitation, stating that much as he would like to revisit Britain, which he had not visited since his school and university days there, and where he had many friends, he would strongly condemn the practice to taking round a few privileged persons on such luxury flights. He therefore refused to participate in it.

Dutt said this practice has been defended on grounds of public relations. But he wondered in reality to what extent this purpose is served. Such practice Dutt regarded it as most unfortunate and contrary to the basic philosophy of public sector. He said sometimes it was argued that this style of functioning has little impact on the cost of production of sizeable undertaking. Dutt argues it is not the cost but the impact it creates on the society and the wasteful spending of public money when resources are scarce in the country.

It was also a practice then in large public enterprises, which used to do block booking in several Indian Airlines flights originating from Delhi to various destination where their plants are located. This used to deny needy passengers of tickets in those flights. These block bookings were utilized for top executives to go to such destinations to attend private functions like a wedding in the family. This was the type of misuse that was prevalent then at the cost of exchequer.

Such practices resulted in public opinion going against the functioning of some of the Public enterprises where there were glaring examples of wasteful expenditure. This made policy makers to think and look back. Obviously government and public enterprises had to begin taking steps to curb such activities so that there was some semblance of austerity. As Government gave more autonomy to

Public enterprises, it made the management more accountable so that wasteful expenditure curbed and profit increased.

Also functioning of public enterprises came under greater scrutiny by Parliament as demand for greater autonomy became vigorous. COPU came out with several critical reports on the performance of public enterprises in 1970s and 1980s. It passed strictures on galloping rise in foreign tours of PSU officials draining the companies resources, unfair pricing policy for certain commodities like raw jute, mismanagement in organisation, administration and financial matters, unusually high expenditure by public sector undertakings for their head offices, extravagant expenditure on guest houses and entertainment and so on. Some political bosses too exploited public enterprises. Some top executives too curried favours to their political bosses.

There were several positive achievements during the 1980s. One significant aspect was the expansion of Unit Trust of India throughout 1980s giving that much additional financial muscle for funding of government projects. The UTI set up in 1964, after the Chinese War had consolidated its position from 1974-1981. From 1981-87, it witnessed significant expansion with launch of various new schemes. With additional tax exemption in 1982-83, it received further fillip. It is creditable and a national pride for any financial institution that it grew from zero unit capital in 1964 to a spectacular figure of Rs 4222.80 crore over 24 years. It became at that time the foremost financial and investment institution among the developing countries and ranked high among the unit trusts and mutual funds in the developed world. But subsequently in the late 1990s and early 2000 it collapsed due to certain mismanagement and hence subsequently the company had to be reorganised.

With Public enterprises growing in size, the problems also increased particularly those concerning industrial relations. But none can question the predominant role of public sector in national development in the first three decades after independence. With lofty goals bestowed on public sector chief executives in face of the growth of the economy, there was increasing responsibilities for effective leadership in improving production, productivity, profits and modernisation of PSUs. As globalisation took firm roots, Public sector had to keep pace with international development to become futuristic industries. This led to increasing demands on financial, managerial and manpower resources. As many countries embarking upon major economic reforms, the debate on private sector versus public sector became sharper.

An advisory committee on programme implementation that went into ills of public sector at that time felt that practically all the PSUs were over-manned resulting in low-productivity-based enterprises and consequently they became dependent on subsidies. For example Air India, which was separate from Indian Airlines at that time had more than 17000 employees operating only 20 aircraft as against 9000 staff flying 38 planes with Singapore Airlines. There were cost escalation and time overrun in 290 projects being implemented by PSUs at that time. Also the technologies were outdated in PSU, which required bold steps for modernisation. Many Psus were heavily loaded with government officials and board did not enjoy autonomy required for efficient functioning. According to Raj K. Nigam, formerly of bureau of public enterprises and an authority of public enterprises, quoted scope to say that public enterprises have succumbed to the influence and authority of the BPE, which was to be a friend, philosopher and guide for the PSUs but has turned out to be another power lever of the government control over them. There was need for PSUs to have self-regulating guidelines drawn up by their own body. Nigam also emphasised the crying need for a White paper on PSUs by the government but with the turn of events and liberalisation of the economy in 1991, this demand never saw the light of the day. SCOPE however came up with its own blueprint on PSUs subsequently.

CHAPTER 6

1990s Watershed Decade for India's Economic Development and Public Enterprises

Manmohan Singh, who was finance minister and architect in P V Narasimha Rao government that embarked upon far reaching economic reforms, quoted Victor Hugo in his first budget speech to say: "No power on earth can stop an idea whose time has come." Singh used this famous quote to drive home the point that though India faced a severe balance of payment crisis, there is no question of looking back and that the economy can only leapfrog from here. Truly, the major economic crisis was converted into opportunity and economy for the first time moved towards average 7 per cent high growth path, which was sustained in subsequent decades to take over 300 million people out of poverty and create an additional 300 million middle class.

ECONOMY FREED FROM SHACKLES OF CONTROLS THROUGH REFORMS

The 1990s could be described as watershed decade in India's economic development. Far reaching reforms were launched in 1991 freeing the economy from the shackles of controls. The economic compulsions triggered it as fiscal deficit rose to 8 per cent of GDP and balance of payment crisis loomed large with foreign exchange reserves enough to meet just two weeks of imports. But this major challenge was converted into an opportunity by Prime Minister P V Narasimha Rao, whose centenary year is being celebrated in 2020. PVN-

Manmohan Singh combine changed face of Indian economy for the better. The significant aspect is that India did not miss the bus to take off and move on to a higher growth trajectory. Drastic reforms were carried out despite resistance from a section of the political class. India never looked back and reforms launched by the government of the day was carried forward by successive government s though some nuances might have changed. Reforms have come to stay and it is by and large irreversible. It started with a big bang in 1991 and subsequently it has become incremental fine-tuning to the changing requirement. Perhaps reforms in Chinese economy in 1979 and the collapse of Soviet Union contributed to the change in the government thinking. The fiscal profligacy indulged in the previous five years pushed the economy towards a debt trap forcing India to think afresh.

The lurking fear against foreign investment was there at that time of independence, particularly after the experience of East India Company, which came in the 18th century to do business and ultimately ended up colonising India. So the emphasis in the first four decades after independence was on self reliance and import substitution, which pursued even today. Prime Minister Narendra Modi has repackaged to call it 'make in India' and Atma nirbhar Bharat'.

SELF-RELIANCE DURING PRE 1991 ERA MEANT IMPORT SUBSTITUTION

The aim, prior to liberalization of the economy, was to produce indigenously as many things as possible irrespective of poor technology. This was meant to cater to the huge domestic market and only surplus, if any, was to be exported. As a result, the political class, right from the days of freedom struggle, were averse to opening up of the economy and believed in swadeshi movement. Hence allowing foreign companies to manufacture domestically was always looked with suspicion. Barring a few exceptions, items of mass consumption were not allowed to be manufactured without majority control by an Indian partner.

But severe debt crisis in the late 1980s, inward looking policy, mounting fiscal deficit and depleting foreign exchange reserves forced the government to have a re-look at its economic policies. Prime Minister P. V. Narasimha Rao addressing one of the apex chamber meetings said it was essential to open up the economy in the given situation but it did not mean that the economic policy pursued in the past was wrong. Socialistic pattern of development was a requirement in the initial stages of development. It laid a strong foundation for the economy to leapfrog by creating the much needed industrial base, particularly that of basic industries. So neither the economic reforms being carried out now nor the socialistic pattern of development pursued earlier were contradictory or wrong. They were in fact the requirement of the given situation to steer an impoverished economy on a growth path.

Several critics at that point of time accused the government of carrying out economic reforms because of the conditions imposed by International Monetary Fund from whom India had to borrow $2.2 billion structural adjustment loan to tide over the balance of payment crisis. The loan might have come with conditionalities but the reforms carried out at that time ensured that India never had to knock at the doors of IMF again. India never borrowed from IMF after that. India not only brought back the gold it had to pledge to prevent defaulting in its global repayment commitments but also brought more gold from IMF subsequently and increased its contribution to IMF to help the multilateral agency lend more to other countries in distress. Countries like Pakistan borrow from IMF even today to tide over balance of payment crisis. India on the other hand not only not borrowed from IMF for nearly three decades, but was sitting pretty with a comfortable foreign exchange reserves of over $500 billion that could meet India's imports of more than a year. India might be accused of succumbing to IMF conditionalities, but the reality is India's reforms were much more and far-reaching to bring about a total change in economic thinking. The fact is India did not succumb but carried a major big ticket reform on its own for a course correction, which some of the political class failed to recognize.

The then Finance Minister Manmohan Singh presented his first budget in July 1991 in which a slew of reform measures were announced. It was followed by a new Industrial Policy Resolution by Prime Minister Narasimha Rao, who himself held the industry portfolio. P Chidambaram, who was minister of state with independent charge in the Commerce Ministry, carried out trade liberalisation through a new EXIM policy. Montek Singh Ahluwalia, who was commerce secretary in Chandra Shekar government, was appointed as Economic Affairs Secretary to assist Manmohan Singh in the finance ministry to carry out reforms. They formed the core team along with S Venkitaramanan first and then C Rangarajan as RBI governor to carry out big bang economic reforms. The reforms were quick and drastic and freed the economy from the slow Hindu rate of growth of 3-3.5 per cent up to 1980 and then at 5-5.5 per cent in the 1980s to higher growth of average seven per cent in the initial years of reforms and at one time before the 2008 global economic crisis, India clocked over 9 per cent for four consecutive years.

The foundation for modern India through the Industrial Policy Resolution of 1948 and 1956 was laid soon after independence. The Industrial Policy was tweaked in subsequent years to meet the emerging challenges in 1973, 1977 and 1980. The 1956 policy laid the foundation for setting up basic and heavy industries in the Public Sector. The 1973 identified high priority industries where large domestic industrial houses and foreign companies could be encouraged to invest. The 1977 policy attempted decentralised development encouraging small scale industries in particular. The 1980 policy made an attempt to encourage foreign investment in high technology areas. A good example is setting up of Maruti Udyog in the joint sector with 50 per cent government equity and 50 per cent equity by the Japanese Suzuki initially. Subsequently with further opening up it became a totally a Japanaese owned Suzuki company.

The Public sector, which has been an important instrument in economic growth of the country since independence, remained an instrument in economic transformation of the country after reforms as well. As ever it played a significant role in the post economic structural readjustment programme with renewed vigour and commitment.

Public sector, which took the economy to commanding height during the era of controls and socialistic pattern of development, remained a major instrument of industrialisation and performed on par with private companies in a liberalised environment taking on the domestic and global competition. Public Enterprises have proved the critics wrong that it would not able to take on the severe competition of private sector in an open economic era. Belying expectations the public sector enterprises barring a few had performed exceedingly well both in terms of efficiency and in discharging social and welfare obligations. In the ranking of the top ten corporates in terms of market capitalisation, six are public enterprises—ONGC, NTPC,SBI, MMTC BHEL and NMDC.

1991 Industrial Policy Reserves Less Number of Sectors for PSUs

The 1991 Industrial Policy resolution reduced number of sectors reserved for public enterprises to 8 from 17 previously. Opening of the economy originally started in the Mid 1980 but they were piecemeal and not comprehensive. The 1991 Industrial Policy which laid the road map for rapid industrialization keeping abreast with the latest available technology unlike in the past when India went for obsolete and second hand technology.

The 1991 Industrial policy Resolution was no exception as far as pursuing self-reliance was concerned. But the difference was it laid greater emphasis on building capacity to pay for imports through foreign exchange earnings. If a company acquired foreign technology, it acquired it by earning foreign exchange through exports over a period of time. This also ensured that India's merchandise and services two-way trade which accounted for hardly $50-60 billion in 1991 grew manifold and it grew close to around $ one trillion. Lately there is some slippages in the face of corona virus pandemic and the ensuing global recession.

PSU Industrial Foundation Helped to Push Growth

The economic kick-start happened rapidly after reforms because of the foundation laid by the public sector. Also the policy makers ensured that India remained domestic market driven economy even though exports played an increasing role. This strategy gave enough cushions to deal with global crisis, unlike in several other emerging economies.

A lot of new and innovative steps were taken including off-loading of government equity in public sector units during the course of the decade to tone up the functioning of public sector. This is the start of disinvestment process, which took the form of strategic sale during NDA government led by Atal Bihari Vajpayee. The strategic sale concept was reversed when Manmohan Singh became Prime Minister following pressure from left parties, who accused the government of attempting to sell family silver to pay the grocers' bill. Prime minister Narendra Modi government is now contemplating outright sale of PSUs including Air India. Manmohan Singh was in favour of outright sale of only those Psus which were patently unviable like Scooters India Ltd.

In the initial stages of disinvestment by Narasimha Rao government, the attempt was to help government garnering some resources to check the burgeoning fiscal deficit in the face of difficult times apart from trying to tone up functioning of PSUs, which happens automatically with stake sale of small percentage of shares. In fact subsequently learning from the experiences, successive governments decided to get practically all the PSUs listed in stock exchange and off-load some minimum percentage of shares in a bid to improve accountability, efficiency and performance.

1991 Industrial Policy Unleashed Entrepreneurship

The 1991 Industrial Policy Resolution unleashed the entrepreneurship among public enterprises. It made public sector to change by shedding laid back approach typical of government organizations. Government also gradually abolished the monopoly of any sector or any individual enterprise excepting in defence manufacturing. The Policy however ensured that some of the noble and cherished goals of the original objectives like encouraging development of backward regions, removing regional imbalances and encouraging small scale industries were not diluted.

This ensured that the industrial policy built on the gains already made in the economy while correcting distortions and weaknesses in the system. It also ensured that reforms were carried out with a human face as then finance minister and later Prime Minister Manmohan Singh described it. This helped in building consensus amongst the political class, who were generally averse to reforms in the early stages. Also consensus building ensured that economic reforms acquired acceptability in most of the political parties barring left parties making liberalisation process irreversible in subsequent years. The pace of reforms might have been slow at times, but they were never reversed in the country during the last 30 years including the controversial decision to open up multi-brand retail to foreign direct investment. The difficult India-US civilian nuclear deal, that helped in building mega nuclear power plants in the country, too went through in 2008 despite stiff opposition from left parties.

To encourage both public and private sector including cooperatives and small scale industries, the new policy was continuity with change and the series of initiatives to boost growth and competition were taken. They included abolition of industrial licensing without impinging upon national interests. The industrial licensing was abolished for all industries barring certain specified industries. The policy freed Indian industry including public sector from the shackles of controls so as to promote foreign investment. This helped in acquiring foreign expertise in marketing, modern managerial techniques, exports and ushering in sophisticated and contemporary technology in manufacturing. It goes to the credit of Prime Minister Narasimha Rao, who sold the reforms even to hawks saying the government was only adopting the middle path. Also he made it gradual and step-by-step approach so that there was general acceptance as people could witness the betterment of the economy on their own.

NEW APPROACH TO PSUS IN THE NEW INDUSTRIAL POLICY

The new policy adopted new approach to public sector. It made public sector growth oriented and technically dynamic. It encouraged restructuring of faltering public enterprises. While public sector was not barred from entry in to any sector, it was made to become competitive to do well. However some areas were continued to be reserved for public sector like essential infrastructure goods and services, oil and mineral exploration and exploitation, technology development and manufacturing in areas where private investment is inadequate or not forthcoming and manufacture of strategic items. Subsequently oil and gas exploration was opened up to private sector. Now mining and mineral development too is opened up. Government also decided to strengthen those public enterprises in reserved and high priority areas. Public sector was provided more management autonomy to enable it earn reasonable profits. The system of memoranda of understanding introduced for public enterprises so as to ensure targets set were achieved year after year. A roadmap was evolved to deal with patently unviable and sick public enterprises.

Along with phased elimination of License-Inspector-Permit raj in the new industrial policy, investment decisions by companies were facilitated by ending restrictions under MRTP Act. The draconian Foreign Exchange Regulation Act (FERA) was replaced by more sober Foreign Exchange Management Act (FEMA) to encourage foreign investment. Most of the foreign exchange violations by companies were criminal offences under FERA but in FEMA they became civil offences thereby diluting punishment for violations. Also India moved away from an era of restrictions in foreign exchange to management of foreign exchange.

With the abolition of MRTP Act, companies did not require government permission to issue shares and for extending their area of operation or establishment of new unit.

The new Trade policy announced by the government as part of the economic reforms freed foreign trade from several unnecessary controls and regulations in one go. Restrictions on exports and imports virtually disappeared barring a few items. Export-Import tax was abolished. It did exist in some limited number of items but at minimum level. Import-Export procedures were simplified. Quantitative restrictions on trade were phased out. Quota system in trade was virtually phased out with the option to exercise it in unusual situations. Foreign exchange market was established where sale and purchase of foreign currency could be done in the open. Import duty on gold was drastically reduced eliminating smuggling thereby several transactions became clean. Government moved towards full convertibility of rupee. Rupee was made fully convertible in the current account by 1994 to facilitate international trade. But on capital account the liberalisation was gradual. The movement towards full convertibility of rupee in the capital account slowed down a bit due to East Asian currency meltdown in 1997 but in subsequent years it picked up. There are still some restrictions in the face of global financial crisis of 2008. This liberal foreign trade policy helped several public sector companies to go global and look up to exports as part of their expansion.

A significant aspect of the new industrial policy was to totally discourage nationalisation of sick private industries, which was done earlier to protect employment. These taken-over sick industries had become a burden to the government and these units accounted for more than one third of the losses of public enterprises in 1991. Also takeover of sick units were not in tune with the original philosophy of public sector.

Along with new Industrial policy, fiscal and monetary reforms were carried out. India had very high fiscal deficit of 8 per cent of GDP during the 1991 crisis. This meant that government was spending more than what it earned by way of taxes. One of the aspects of containing fiscal deficit was to increase income through tax reforms. Global experience has shown lower the taxes higher the compliance, thereby the tax net was widened and revenue collections improved resulting in government having more money for implementing socio-economic programmes apart from improving the fiscal health of the economy. Also, companies, particularly public enterprises were able to carry out their expansion programmes through internal generation of resources and debt rather than depending upon budgetary support from the government.

Some overzealous reformists at times started comparing performance of public and private sectors. Federation of Indian Chambers of Commerce and industry, championing the cause of private sector came out with a study to suggest that the losses of public sector between 1985 and 1997 totalled a little over Rs two lakh crore, which was a huge sum those days. A deeper analysis revealed that this study was a classic case of part distortions and part twisted conclusions. To arrive at this pre-conceived conclusion, the FICCI study had excluded the oil sector and financial institutions like State Bank of India and Industrial Development Bank of India. While FICCI study overlooked a large number of public sector corporates, it included several sick and bankrupt private sector companies taken over by the government. For example over 100 sick textiles mills were nationalised by government in the 1970s to protect the interest of the workers. Also there were distortions of profit figures of some of the public sector undertakings. The FICCI study lost sight of the fact that the public sector was not promoted basically to earn profits. Unfortunately FICCI debate focused only on financial parameters.

Since FICCI study was totally one sided and distorted, Center for Industrial and Economic Research was commissioned by Standing Conference of Public Enterprises to carry out an objective study on performance and public and private sectors in the country based on empirical facts. A comparative analysis of financial results by CIER study of top 50 and top 100 public and private sector companies in 1997-98 showed that two segments came close to each other. In number of cases the public sector logged better results. Against RONW, return on net worth, of 11.9 per cent of the top 50 private companies, the comparative top public enterprises registered 13 per cent return, a full one per cent higher. The divergence gets reduced with the extension of the horizon from top 50 to top 100 corporates. Yet it is the public sector which scores higher 11.9 per cent to 11.3 per cent of private sector.

According to a study paper by Confederation of Indian Industry, which was quoted by CIER study said Tatas stood at a position much below Gas Authority of India. Almost three quarters of the private companies actually eroded shareholder value.

Analysis of data produced by the Center for Monitoring Indian Economy, spanning some two-thirds of the organised industrial sector, showed that public sector enterprises produced better results than did the private sector, be it contribution to the national exchequer, growth in capital formation or in operating profit, dividend to net worth, administrative efficiency or value added. In several other parameters, it compared favourably. Where it did not, the divergence was marginal.

The CIER empirical study sponsored by SCOPE to expose the fallacies by examining relevant facts came to the unmistakable conclusion that there has been considerable amount of disinformation about the performance public sector, a part of which is faulty understanding of history, role and objectives of public enterprises, and a part deliberate effort to run it down. Biased studies published and frequent statements made have contributed to the prevailing ambience. Ever since independence several public sector companies have had performance comparable to the best in the world. A great deal of adverse understanding of the public sector stemmed from its old image, which was evolving itself through experimentation. Some yet to be defined ideas and lofty ideals about building a new society from the debris of backwardness of development prevailed. While the public sector was supposed to be the engine of growth and an instrument of state policies and the much needed empowerment was conspicuous by its absence, high profits has emerged, at the end of the day, as the litmus test, CIER study observed.

Notwithstanding the fears expressed in various quarters that public sector will meet its waterloo with the liberalisation of the economy, the performance of central public sector post 1991 showed steady improvement. The gross margin in capital employed has risen from 17.9 per cent in 1990-91 to 23.6 per cent in 1997-98. Similarly,

PAT/equity ratio that is, profit after tax to equity, had escalated to 20.9 per cent in 1997-98. The return grew impressively from 8 per cent in 1990-91 to 29.4 per cent in 1997-98. Ten case studies of ten star performing central public sector companies established that public enterprises have not only performed well but also managed better than private sector. Indian Oil was the only Fortune 500 company from India in the late 1990s. ONGC and BHEL and NTPC have consistently performed well and they have come to be recognised all over the World. IPCL then a PSU, VSNL another PSU then, Engineers India, Power Finance Corporation are some of other well performing and managed companies.

Armed with these records of excellence, these performers demolish many a myth, which is associated with or attributed to the public sector. The study also demonstrates unequivocally that, given the freedom of operations and without being loaded with commercially exogenous baggage, a public sector organisation can perform as well as any other anywhere.

The reform measures helped the economy to grow at a faster pace and public sector too benefitted. Systemic changes brought about like introduction of MOUs and Navratna dispensation that is categorisation of Public Enterprises on the basis of their performances helped them expand in the face of increased profits. Public enterprises modernised their operations which resulted in reduction in their manpower. Between 1990-91 and 2007-08, public enterprises profits after tax increased 35 times and their turnover increased nine times. Most of the expansion was done through generation of internal resources. In fact competition had improved their performance.

Disinvestment of public enterprises formed an important component of economic reforms. It had many dimensions like privatisation, injecting competition, overcoming budget constraints, financial sector reforms, changes in foreign currency management, changing relations between government and public enterprises management. The idea behind reforms is to ensure the entire system geared itself to market economy and be quick to adopt changing market situation and competition. For this public enterprises had to become more efficient, reduce influence of trade unions and minimise the drain on resources and burden on the state. There is no uniform pattern in the reform strategy of public sector. Different countries adopted different strategies. India and China opened up its economies much before off-loading government equity in public sector. In case of India, initially bundling of shares of some profit making public enterprises along with some loss making and sick units were done so as to sell them as a package. This did not work well. So government adopted sale of small percentage of shares in installment in some profit making public enterprises so as to have better acceptance in the equity market for off-loading of government shares. Then NDA government led by Atal Bihari Vajpayee adopted more liberal approach. It privatized a few public enterprises and resorted to strategic sale of at least 26 per cent stake in some others. Some cross holding by cash rich oil public enterprises was attempted to meet fiscal deficit requirement without the government equity going into private hands. This approach of big ticket disinvestment was not appreciated by general public and opposition parties which accused the government of selling family silver for paying grocers' bill.

Subsequently when Congress led UPA government came to power with left parties outside support, it was decided as part of the common minimum programme not to off-load government equity beyond 49 per cent in any government owned enterprises so that public sector character is retained. Since then disinvestment to the present day has been to ensure public sector character of the state enterprises. Of course in the case of sick units attempt would be first made to revive the company and only when it became patently unviable and turnaround not possible, outright sale of those companies would be attempted. This policy is now being changed by Narendra Modi government. This change is perhaps required now to inject competition and perhaps to bring about turnaround and open up more areas and companies for acquisition by private companies. This will help in unlocking value of several public enterprises. Public enterprises also have huge parcel of land and entering into joint venture with multinationals will help in bringing in more investments as well as technology.

Taking cue from British experience of privatisation of public enterprises, Latin American countries like Argentina and Chile liberalised and deregulated the economy along with privatisation of public enterprises. In East Asia, the trend has been to off-load minority stake in public enterprises just as in the case of India in the past so that public sector character is not lost. Some of the Latin American economies and South East Asian economies, which rapidly made their currencies fully convertible on capital account had to pay a heavy price during East Asian currency meltdown, which virtually depleted their foreign exchange reserves resulting in rapid and unsustainable depreciation of their currency and hyper inflation putting their economy in severe distress. India's approach of encouraging public sector helped in staving off economic crisis both during 1997 currency meltdown and 2008 global financial crisis.

With the liberalisation of the economy, strategies were evolved to deal with sickness in public enterprises. A collaborative study by SCOPE and CIER PSU sickness demolished the perception that central public enterprises had not performed well in terms of financial parameters. A more informed assessment led to the conclusion that given a level-playing measure of performance, the public sector has produced and possessed the capacity to produce comparable results. Industrial sickness was not an exclusive prerogative of central public enterprises. The number of sick private enterprises exceeded 270,000 in March 1996 as per Reserve Bank of India study. As many as 2254 references have been made to BIFR as of June 1998. Of these 2098 were from private sector. BIFR had ordered winding up of 27 per cent of these companies and revival of 19 per cent of them.

At the turn of the century various strategies were also worked out to deal with sickness in public enterprises. They included disinvestment, restructuring, modernisation and even closure of patently unviable sick public enterprises. One problem that came in the way of dealing with sickness both in public and private sector particularly after economic reforms injected competition was labour reforms. That part of economic reforms has been painfully slow in India as necessary and meaningful social safety net is yet to be created in the country. Any labour reforms including hire and fire system can be implemented only when there are adequate social security and retraining available to retrenched workers. This involved adequate financial resources and wherewithal of skill development. Without these being put in place, a meaningful labour reforms cannot take place particularly in a democracy where it had be done with a human face.

Chapter 7

Public Enterprises Change for Better with Increasing Disinvestment in 21st Century

Late K C Pant as Deputy Chairman of Planning Commission during NDA government led by Atal Bihari Vajpayee said in an interview to SCOPE run monthly magazine Kaleido Scope: "the objectives of disinvestment programme are not only to reduce fiscal deficit as it is commonly perceived, but also to improve the performance of PSEs, improve their professionalism, subject them to market discipline, encourage wider public participation, promote greater accountability and thus improve their competitiveness."

This sums up the thinking of the government at the turn of the century as the public sector witnessed turbulent times. With the growing phenomenon of privatisation in the world, India was no exception as this thinking influenced the then Government.

Though the previous Narasimha Rao government, which carried out drastic economic reforms in 1991 and went overdrive on freeing the economy from the shackles of controls, it remained committed to retaining public sector character. It had started the disinvestment process but committed to not selling more than 20 per cent stake in any of the enterprises barring perhaps patently sick public enterprises that could not be revived.

Government Philosophy on Public Enterprises Changes

In 1998 the Vajpayee government, which came to power, however, decided on a big bang reforms on public sector and pursued privatisation policy and strategic sale of PSEs. This led to sharp criticism from various quarters sparking off a public outrage.

World over public sector was being dismantled rapidly starting with Britain in the late 1970s and there was systematic disinformation about public sector that its performance was low and highly inefficient and that private sector was resource-efficient. With this fallacy spreading like wildfire in India and that too the government started carrying out a crusade against public sector. But empirical study by Standing Conference of Public Enterprises came to the fore to prevent outright dismantling of public sector.

The study established that the public sector was in no way less efficient than private sector and fully geared to meet the challenges of reforms if restructured and given the requisite freedom and autonomy. Even in the given circumstances public sector performed better than private sector despite the non-level playing field. Also public sector was no longer that of yesteryears and it was changing with the time by itself to take on competition.

The SCOPE led study and expert opinions compared macro level evaluation and followed it with ten public sector case studies. The studies indicate that given the necessary freedom of governance, public sector can achieve greater heights than private sector. Also the analysis showed that the success of public sector is not limited to the ten star performers alone.

The study indicated that the ten private sector enterprises, which belonged to or are considered outstanding management groups or corporate have performed poorly when compared to the top ten PSUs. This exploded the myth of the invincibility of the private sector. There were many multiple failures in private sector as well. Also failure in private sector was not limited to a few selective cases. Besides the study indicated that private sector failures have not only failed as commercial enterprises but there were many more defaulters and perpetrated acts of omission and commission, which do not merely erode shareholders value but which impact heavily on the interests of other stakeholders including significant public interests. At that time CII too conducted performance study of 165 top public and private sector companies in India. It found top performers amongs them were public sector.

Detractors of public sector also argued that public sector profits were dominated by oil companies. The SCOPE study established that other public sector companies too performed well and the drag on public sector were mostly private sick industries taken over by public sector. There were some laggards in public sector but their percentage was no different from that of private sector.

DISINVESTMENT COMMISSION SET UP

A disinvestment commission headed by G V Ramakrishna was set up in 1996 to examine withdrawal of public sector from non-core and non-strategic areas. The Commission gave its recommendations in 1999. It studied 58 enterprises referred to it and suggested strategic sale for 29 of them. Earlier in 1992 a committee headed by C Rangrajan, former RBI Governor, was set up to institutionalise disinvestment process. It had made more drastic recommendation that government should hold 51 per cent or more equity only in industries explicitly reserved for public sector like coal and lignite, mineral oils, arms and ammunition, defence equipment, atomic and railway transport. In exceptional cases in other industries where the enterprise had dominant share, the government can keep 26 per cent equity and divest up to 74 per cent. In all other cases the public enterprises should be privatized up to 100 per cent. These recommendations hardly got political support that too in the early stages of reforms. There was therefore hardly any taker for such far-reaching recommendations. Rao government did not as he was pursuing other more important reform agenda. Vajpayee government decided to take up this unfinished reform agenda.

Unmindful of the growing public outcry, the trigger for big ticket disinvestment was made in the budget speech in Parliament in 2000-01. The then Finance Minister Yashwant Sinha said the government policy on public sector is that it will restructure and revive potentially viable PSUs but would close down PSUs which cannot be revived. The government would bring down equity in all non-strategic PSUs to 26 per cent or lower if necessary. He also recommended bringing down government equity to 33 per cent in public sector banks. These drastic measures have not happened till date.

This led to heated debate in Parliament on government's disinvestment policy during which NDA government was floored by the opposition. The attack on the government was spearheaded by Mani Shankar Aiyer of Congress and Basudeb Acharia of CPI (M). The opposition demolished the government argument for privatisation and widely quoted the SCOPE's empirical study, which brought out clearly the facts about superiority of public sector over private sector. The comparative study showed public sector performed better in several or perhaps all the important parameters and the need of the hour is to restructure to perform even better rather than privatising them. The opposition then was not against disinvestment but was against privatisation, which it described as selling family silver to pay the grocers bill.

The government however argued that the big ticket disinvestment plan was conceived because in 2001-02, 119 profit making enterprises earned a total net profit 36432 crore and 109 loss making enterprises incurred a loss of Rs 10387 crore. So the total profit earned by 230 central public enterprises was just Rs 26045 crore. The major part of PSU profits came from oil PSUs. If oil PSUS are excluded the rate of return on capital employed was very low. Of course investment in PSUs cannot be seen merely from profit point of view as there were certain social objectives needed to be fulfilled, particularly in the early stages of development. In early 2000 it was felt that PSUs needed to improve their technical efficiency that is the productivity of inputs. The government therefore decided to set up separate department of disinvestment and later a separate disinvestment ministry. First it was headed by Arun Jaitley and later by Arun Shourie.

The government then decided that the money earned through disinvestment and privatisation was to be utilized for spending in social sectors, restructuring of PSUs or retiring public debt. But this was not fully implemented. Government however claimed at that time that the money spent on social programmes was from consolidated fund of India, where the disinvestment proceeds too went in. As the money spent on social programmes was more than the money it received from disinvestment proceeds, the money did actually go into social programmes. However this argument has not been accepted by critics, who said the money on social programmes were already planned and budgeted and hence no addition was made to it following the additional revenue from disinvestment.

Sale of loss making PSU was contemplated to reduce the budgetary support being provided to such units, which was increasingly becoming a drain on exchequer. The progress of disinvestment in India has been very slow, considering the strides in privatisation in other emerging economies. According to the World Bank (Global Development Finance) 2000, earnings from privatisation in all developing countries totaled 272 billion dollars in the 1990s till 1998. Of this India's share was seven billion dollars. Except for three years (1991-92, 1994-95 and 1998-99), the budget targets for disinvestment were not met. Between 1991-92 and 1999-2000, the total realisation was Rs. 18,368 crore against the targeted Rs. 44,300 crore. The Government had divested a part of Central PSUs ranging from about 2 per cent to 49 per cent in forty undertakings till March 1999. The largest chunk of over 40 per cent of government equity had been divested in Hindustan Petroleum Corporation, Videsh Sanchar Nigam, Mahanagar Telephone Nigam, Indian Petrochemicals Corporation and Hindustan Organic Chemicals.

The Prime Minister's Economic Advisory Council in a report on Economic Reforms later suggested that where PSUs cannot function as commercial organisations, not able to compete with other private sector units and with imports, they should be sold to the public or financial institutions or to a strategic private investor. The resources realised from the sale of equity could be more profitably deployed in building essential infrastructure or in retiring public debt, it said. The Economic Survey of the Union Government (2000-01) has also emphasized the need to get the Government out of the business of production and enhance its presence and performance in the provision of public goods (basic infrastructure, education, health etc). Funds from privatisation would also help to reduce public debt and bring down the debt-GDP ratio while competitive public enterprises would be enabled to function effectively.

In 1999-2000, the NDA government has been criticised by experts for adopting two different approaches for sale of shares in two oil marketing companies. In the case of BPCL, the government adopted public offering methodology while in HPCL, the shares were offloaded to strategic investor. This resulted in criticism that the government replaced public monopoly by private monopoly through disinvestment and privatisation. The example, often cited are, strategic sale of VSNL to Tatas and IPCL to Reliance. There were also criticism by CAG and Public Accounts Committee regarding undervaluation of shares in privatisation and strategic sale of PSU companies. Modern Foods India was the first case of privatisation in January 2000 in which 74 per cent of government equity was divested to strategic partner with management control. This was followed by strategic sale in BALCO in March 2001 and then Computer Maintenance Corporation, Hindustan Teleprinters, IBP, VSNL, Pradeep Phosphates and Hindustan Zinc in 2001-02 and Maruti Udyog and IPCL in May 2002. Some of the ITDC Hotels were sold outright from November 2001 to July 2002.

The controversy over the privatisation and the attempted resale of Centaur Hotel, located near Mumbai's airport at Santa Cruz, has highlighted the flawed manner in which public sector undertakings are valued before being put up for sale. It also indicated the worst form of crony capitalism and the then Disinvestment Minister Arun Shourie came under sharp criticism.

Justifying the government's stand, Shourie said in Parliament during the forceful debate on disinvestment that government had spent Rs 34,000 crore for 23 revival packages, an amount of about Rs.35,500 crore has been spent, but not one unit is revived, as yet.

Basudeb Acharia debunked this argument saying the money spent on public sector was inadequate and hence they are not getting revived. Also the money got from disinvestment is not going into revival of public enterprises but utilised for bridging the fiscal deficit. He also cited the example of Modern Food and said selling of land as in NTC would have resulted in more value than outright sale. Privatisation is not the only panacea for ills of public sector. There are several examples of loss making public sector turning around to make profits.

Mani Shankar Aiyar, another strong advocate of public sector said his congress party regarded disinvestment as part of economic reform but certainly not the heart of reforms. For the BJP and the NDA, however, disinvestment has emerged as the central plank of their platform of reforms. Before embarking on a policy that will deprive the nation of national control, over Rs.65,000 crore of national equity, Rs. 2.5 lakh crore of national investment and some Rs. 10 to 15 lakh crore of national assets, surely this Parliament has a right to White Paper which sets out the rationale for the wholesale auction of national wealth.

"We need a White Paper, which answers at least the following basic questions. Which are the sectors in which the Government regards a continuing public sector presence, as essential. Which are the public units that should be run on purely commercial basis. How should strategic industries, be defined. What constitutes a crore industry. Our manufacturing PSEs should be treated on par, with those in the service sector. Should a distinction be made between the PSUs that pioneered new fields of industrialisation and the PSUs which resulted from the failure of the private sector to run their enterprises. On what criteria should management control be transferred and under what circumstances would the transfer of ownership be permitted? What objective criteria – should be put in place to determine whether a given unit should or should not be disinvested. On what criteria the units should be rehabilitated, revived, restructured? Should not one distinguish between profit-making and loss-making PSUs? Whether Navratnas should be exempted from disinvestment? What should be the modalities for disinvestment for different categories of PSUs? What should be done with the proceeds of disinvestment? What steps need to be taken urgently and as a matter of high national priority to render public sector undertakings functionally autonomous? We do not seek ad hoc answers to this question. We want a policy. A disinvestment programme without a Disinvestment Policy is an invitation to suspicion of your motives," he said.

"It seems that the Government have unleashed an ideological assault on the public sector that have a little bearing on our social and political realities or larger national goals. We are told that the public sector is an unbearable burden on the public exchequer. I fail to see how," he said

"There is no single factor that has contributed more to public sector woes than the drastic scaling down by the then government. The other argument for the Government's flight from the public sector is that the public sector is inherently incapable of making itself efficient. But how is it that in 18 successive public global tenders. BHEL has without fail beaten multinational giants, like ABB, Seimens and GEC Alsthom? Did not the same SAIL which made a loss of Rs.1600 crore under the NDA Government, made a profit of Rs.1300 crore in subsequent years. Also public sector losses are modest in most cases and large only in a few. DRDO and ISRO are among the most outstanding of their kind in the world. GAIL has never been beaten by British Gas. Curiously, of the 10 most profitable public sector units, the Government has disinvested or proposed to disinvest its holdings in as many as eight. But the ten top loss-making units only three or four are being disinvested. The Government says, it needs the resources. We asked resources for what? Is it to fund the fiscal deficit? I find it shocking that Arun Shourie should draw the attention to the net worth of Modern Foods having been a mere Rs.28 crore. Why then did the Hindustan Levers cough up Rs.105 crore to buy a net worth that is a third of their investment? Is it because they have re-evaluated the replacement value of the physical and commercial assets of different unit of Modern Foods as being above Rs.1000 crore? Let the private sector and the MNCs enter areas reserved hitherto for the public sector and let the public sector compete with the private sector.

A Minister who believes the public sector is inherently inefficient is clearly not a Minister to be trusted with the public sector. This Minister has no faith in Swadeshi, Swabhiman and Swavalamban. We demand a White Paper in which the Government is free to substantiate the Minister's claim that public sector undertakings are inherently inefficient. Until then call a halt to this squandering of the people's wealth in this mindless pursuit of disinvestments," Mani Shankar Aiyer said.

With such raging controversies surfacing, the Congress led UPA government, which came to power in 2004 with Manmohan Singh as Prime Minister, abandoned the policy of strategic sale and privatisation and reverted to the earlier policy of disinvestment in which government equity will not be diluted beyond 51 per cent. The UPA government also made it clear that public sector banks too will retain its public sector character. Government will hold majority share of at least 51 per cent even though banks were allowed to off-load government stake periodically to raise capital from the market.

Also with the economy clocking over 9 per cent growth since 2004 until global financial crisis of 2008 resulted in economic slowdown, the disinvestment process too slowed down a bit with government's fiscal situation improving and left parties in particular, an ally of UPA averse to the very idea of privatisation. Left parties also insisted on government creating a fund from the sale proceeds of government equity in PSUs, which could be utilised for revival of sick PSUs and for social schemes to fulfil stringent RBI's prudential norms dictated by Basel banking guidelines.

With government's revenue buoyancy partly arising out of higher growth and because of top public sector undertakings generating huge surpluses, the strategic sale route was slowly abandoned. More and more empirical evidence of performance of public and private enterprises emerged. The belief that private enterprises should be more efficient than public enterprises was waning. In a situation where market power is significant natural monopolies like power and water utilities, there appeared to be no efficiency difference between public and private firms. In competitive environment too public enterprises is not always less efficient. Public enterprises operating in markets where they have market power, they do as well as private enterprises. When markets are deregulated, the performance of both public and private improves. Going by these empirical evidence there are well run as well as badly run firms in both public and private sector.

Public sector has always come to the rescue of government, be it in the early days of independence or an era of shortages and crisis situation. It has also contributed to government kitty by way of dividend payouts, tax revenue or disinvestment proceeds. Oil companies have shared the subsidy burden of the government particularly when global oil prices skyrocketed. Most of the patently unviable public enterprises are those sick units taken over by the government to protect jobs in an era when government had employment generation as one of main tasks. Some efficiently run public enterprises like ITI and HMT too became sick because they did not change with changing technology.

PSUs Come under CAG & CVC Scrutiny

During this period public enterprises came under more public scrutiny. Audit by Comptroller and Auditor General (CAG) and vigilance by Central Vigilance Commission were already there but it took more virulent form and public enterprises coming under vigrous scrutiny by these watchdogs during this period as several large public sector undertakings were on an expansion mode with Indian economy growing rapidly. PSUs involved in infrastructure, heavy industries, steel, oil etc were making huge investments and scrutiny became more probing as parliamentarians too took greater interest.

PSUs Comes under RTI

Public enterprises came under Right to Information Act as well in 2005. This put public sector under vigorous public scrutiny but this also helped private sector in the sense that they tried to use RTI to exploit public sector by getting information on their business goals. This resulted in further widening the playing field between public sector and private sector in a competitive environment.

With the opening up of the economy there was a craving for more functional and financial autonomy to public enterprises to compete and take on competition as globalisation spread its tentacles. So government in July 1997 took first path breaking step to public sector reform by uncaging nine.

RATNA STATUS TO PSUs FOR MORE FINANCIAL AND FUNCTIONAL AUTONOMY

PSEs to become globe trotter. Referring to them as "Navratnas", they were granted financial and functional autonomy. The status was given based on their size, performance, nature of activities, future prospects etc.

In October 1997, the government in order to make promising profit making CPSEs more efficient and competitive granted enhanced autonomy and delegation of financial powers. The enterprise having continuous trend of profit earning during the previous three years but were not accorded Navratna status were categorised as Miniratna –I and Miniratna – II based on profit earned.

The Ratna structure was later revised. The government introduced Maharatna scheme in February 2010 with the objective to delegate enhanced powers to the Boards of identified large sized Navratna CPSEs so as to facilitate expansion of their operations, both in domestic as well as global markets. (See brief about Maharatna, Navratna and Miniratna schemes, eligibility criteria, delegation of power and their list in box – I, II & III respectively).

As of November 2015, there were 7 Maharatna public enterprises, 16 Navratnas and 71 Miniratnas. This categorisation has helped these profit making public enterprises take on global competition very well as decision making process on investments got speeded up.

PLAN TO REVIVE SICK PSUs

In September 2004, the government came out with a plan to revive sick public enterprises on the basis of suggestion made by Standing

Conference of Public Enterprises (SCOPE). Prime Minister Manmohan Singh constituted Board for Reconstruction of Public Sector Enterprises (BRPSE). He made the announcement at a conference of CEOs of PSEs organized by SCOPE and Department of Public Enterprises in September 2004. Within four months BRPSE was set up in December 2004 to find ways for revival of sick Central public enterprises. BRPSE has recommended revival, rehabilitation plan in at least 64 PSEs recommended to it. Of these at least 45 have been proposed for revival and the government has accepted the proposal. At least 18 of the units revived, have turned around. They included companies like Bharat Pumps and Compressors, Cement Corporation of India, HEC, Andrew Yule and MECON, BCCI, National Film Development Corporation. Government has closed three public enterprises, which were found to be patently unviable.

Infrastructure required substantial modernisation and expansion in the country with rapid growth of the economy and the government therefore introduced public-private partnership model during the 10th five year plan beginning 2002. This has been pursued in subsequent plans as well. PPP is a partnership between public sector entity, which will be a sponsoring authority, and a private sector entity, a legal entity in which 51 per cent equity or more will be with the private partner. There can be one or more private partner. Under PPP model the management will hold the hands of private partner and the concession period will be on commercial terms. The private partner will be chosen in a transparent manner.

Infrastructure investment was stepped up substantially to $320 billion in the 10th plan with the government embarking upon massive highway development with the launch of golden quadrilateral and government found the resources for it by pooling in with the private sector. The major investment in PPP projects began in Maharashtra around 2002 followed by Karnataka, Madhya Pradesh, Gujarat and Tamil Nadu. This gradually spread to other states and in other sectors like power, ports, airports, irrigation telecommunications, water supply and so on. In the 11th plan beginning 2007, the infrastructure investment was stepped up to

$500 billion and in the ongoing 12th plan beginning 2012, infrastructure investment was stepped up to $1 trillion. The PPP model has been expanded to other sectors as well like education and health. The PPP model has some hiccups and it has been periodically tweaked to meet the emerging challenges. Even today highway projects accounted for over 50 per cent of the PPP projects. Under PPP model, government also provides what is called viability gap funding.

VIABILITY GAP FUNDING

Viability gap funding means a grant, one-time or deferred, provided to support infrastructure projects that are economically justified but fall short of financial viability. The lack of financial viability usually arises from long gestation periods and the inability to increase user charges to commercial levels. Usually VGF is 30 per cent of the project cost, which is borne by the government. In 12th five year plan from 2012-17, nearly 50 per cent of the proposed $1 trillion investment in infrastructure is to be implemented under PPP model. This meant government would be spending $150 billion by way of VGF and get $500 billion worth of infrastructure project implemented under PPP. That is $350 billion will be spent by the private sector in those projects. So government is able to implement three times more investment in infrastructure utilising Viability Gap Fund.

But the PPP model is yet to take off fully as it is still an evolving model. It has not yet stabilised as it is being tweaked periodically on the basis of experience gained. Nevertheless, it is a model with proper fine-tuning could help in stepping up public-private partnership. It can also help unlock value for both public and private sector and at times foreign companies as well, especially with ever increasing inflow of Foreign Direct Investment now over $50 billion annually.

CHAPTER 8

Need to Strengthen PSU was Felt More Soon After 2008 Financial Crisis

Wisdom dawned among experts after the collapse of Soviet Union in 1991 that extreme Marxian philosophy of socialistic pattern of development did not provide answers to all the weaknesses and ills of an economy. Likewise the 2008 global financial crisis also thought a lesson that unbridled free market economy practiced by the capitalist United States did not possess Adam Smith's invisible hand to correct the weaknesses in the economy.

This 2008 global financial crisis has only corroborated India's founding fathers belief that mixed economic pattern of development in the formative years after independence with tilt towards socialistic pattern of development and later with a tilt towards capitalistic, more precisely market oriented, system of development in an era of globalisation was the most preferred sustainable development model. Past experience clearly showed that only mixed economy can weather the storm. It gave the economic strength to face the emerging challenges like currency meltdown like the East Asian crisis, recession, financial crisis and so on.

A Mix of Socialism and Capitalism Needed for Welfare of People

An emerging economy like India needed a mix of socialism widely represented by public sector and social programmes and free market economy to enable private sector contribute to the development process, Both state and civil society are needed for improved and efficient delivery of social schemes as witnessed after the liberalisation of economy in 1991. This mixed economic system has stood the test of time and has been very handy in dealing with difficult situations arising out of external factors, be it wars of 1960s, oil crisis of 1970s, collapse of Soviet Union, 1997 East Asian currency meltdown or 2008 global financial crisis arising out of capitalism. Now the global economic recession due to corona virus pandemic has thought us, social safety net was critical to overcome difficult economic situation.

The World economy has not fully recovered since the 2008 crisis and now when there were green shoots of recovery, the pandemic made it worse pushing global depression worse than that of 1930s.

PUBLIC ENTERPRISES AND PSU BANKS HELP TO TIDE OVER 2008 CRISIS

No country can be insulated from the contagion effect of the crisis but the conservative approach and gradual reform process has ensured that India had a safety valve during the 2008 crisis. This helped the economy recover in view of the macro-economic stability and strong fundamentals. It is noteworthy that public enterprises and public sector banks contribute immensely to mitigate the crisis.

This crisis situation has impacted China as well. China which pursued export-led growth to become a global manufacturing hub is feeling the heat and its economy, which had clocked double-digit growth for over two decades has started slowing rapidly with demand for goods from China falling sharply in Europe and United States. The pandemic has made it worse for China with several countries shying away from Chinese goods. This has made slowdown more rapid and steep.

India too started exporting in a big way after economic reforms to ward off balance of payment crisis as witnessed in 1990-91 and ensure the country earned foreign exchange for its imports. From a stage when India had just enough foreign exchange for just two week imports in 1991 forcing policy makers to go far long awaited economic reforms, the country has come a long way to have a foreign exchange reserves at over $500billion, sufficient to meet almost India's imports for over a year. Also India's merchandise and services exports which together were a mere $20-30 billion yearly in 1991 has grown to nearly $500 billion annually at present. The two way trade is nearly $1 trillion now from about $50 billion in 1991.

But the difference between India and China is that Indian economy still largely dependent on domestic market unlike in China where exports accounted for 50 per cent of its GDP. So, drastic fall in exports meant virtual collapse of the Chinese growth story.

India's growth might not have been as rapid as China's but reforms ensured Indian economy moved to a higher growth path on a sustainable pace. India always had a soft landing in the event of a crisis. Many emerging economies faced hard landing from time to time in times of global economic crisis. Even miracle economies of South East Asia or Latin America had problems because over zeolous pursuits of reforms. India too is increasing exports year after year but its share in GDP is at manageable level unlike in China.

Soviet Union and East European economies brand of socialism, collapsed, but India survived by the timely opening up in 1991. This made India land softly during a crisis and ensured that the transition was smooth. So also when East Asian currency meltdown happened, many miracle economies of South East Asia, South Korea and Latin American countries like Brazil and Argentina collapsed as they rapidly moved towards full convertibility of their respective currencies on Capital Account. Brazil, which had $75 billion foreign exchange reserves at that time, came down drastically to $35 billion in a very short time besides high inflation and fast depreciating currency. India was able to weather the storm as it was gradually moving towards full convertibility of Rupee in capital account.

These empirical evidences are not in too distant past. They clearly indicate that extreme developmental models are not sustainable. The economic growth might have been rapid in those economies, but the collapse too is rapid and hard.

PSUs WERE ROLE MODELS FOR PRIVATE SECTOR IN INDIA

In the early stages of development in India, Public sector played an important role in creating industrial base. During globalisation, public sector geared itself to take on competition and became role models for private companies to emulate. Public Sector was also successful to take on competition from private sector bigwigs and multinational companies.

Today when most of the advanced economies are yet to recover from 2008 financial crisis, India is the fastest growing economy until corona virus pandemic hit the world resulting in most countries going on a tail spin and clocking negative growth.

But India is now the only attractive place for large scale investment when consumer demand is faltering elsewhere. India's consumer demand has dropped sharply due to lockdown but this is temporary and is expected to bounce back on normality returned to the economy. Also, there are expectations that many multinationals may move out of China with several countries including US and Europe rejigging their investment plans and want an alternative to Chinese products. India is likely to be the obvious choice for most of those investments through countries like Vietnam, Bangladesh and South East Asian countries too could attract some.

The huge infrastructure deficit in roads, railways, airports, ports, power and so on has made investments worthwhile as it had the advantage of falling of global commodity prices. Economists usually prescribe massive investments in infrastructure at a time of falling consumer demand in order to kick-start the economy when the recovery starts. This would help the economy to build capacity to take on the demand when it picks up as infrastructure needed for capacity building will not happen overnight. Also many countries like Japan, United States and Canada are looking opportunity to invest abroad to help them come out of recession as their own countries offered very little scope for fresh investments. In Japan interest rates are virtual zero or in the negative and they are looking for investment opportunity long term and are offering loans at very low interest rates and time is ripe for India to attract them by taking up mega rail, road, port projects. Also pension funds in United States and Canada too are scouting for opportunities in countries like India. India should cash-in on this opportunity by taking massive projects across the country so as to pump prime the economy.

If public sector built up basic and heavy industries in early stages of development, it took on competition from private sector after economic reforms. Large public enterprises like ONGC, NTPC, SBI, MMTC BHEL, NMDC and so on were standing tall in front of some new generation private sector giants like Reliance Industries, Bharti Airtel, Infosys and ICICI bank and old generation private sector companies like ITC and Larson and Tubro. Of course there were some failures as well. Companies like ITI and HMT, which set the pace of the economy before liberalisation, failed after 1991 as it did not change with the time and their inability to adopt sophisticated modern technology to take on competition.

Public sector banks played a stellar role during the global financial crisis. The conservative monetary policy pursued by the Reserve Bank of India during 2004-08 ensured that the asset bubble in the making in some of the real sectors in India did not burst but got diffused over a period of time. The signs of over-heating, particularly in the reality sector, were well managed. The global financial crisis and the collapse of global investment banker Lehman Brothers, resulted in US government providing a $85 billion bailout. Subsequently several US banks and companies collapsed as well as some in other advanced countries resulting in an overall bailout package of $4-5 trillion, directly or indirectly. United States, considered to be a front-runner in free market economy, had to nationalise failing business entities and banks. Countries like United States and Britain, a strong votery against nationalisation in the 1980s had to resort to it when crisis struck there, debunking the theory of free market economy.

Western central bankers and multilateral institutions, which had severely criticised the then RBI Governor Y V Reddy (2003-08) for his conservative and hawkish monetery policy, showered unusual praise for his prudent monetery policy that ensured that Indian banks particularly public sector banks accounting for 75 per cent of banking in India, did not collapse and instead had the extra liquidity to provide much needed monetary stimulus to tide over the crisis. Apart from public sector banks, which were well regulated by India's central bank, the country's public enterprises by itself acted as a regulator by providing the much needed deterrent through competition to the industrial sector during the period. This ensured private sector companies and banks too were able to tide over the situation in India. The PPP model, which is now in vogue particularly in the infrastructure development in the country is win-win for both public and private sector. Public sector influence in them ensured that the private sector did not go haywire or berserk by providing the balancing act. A blend of public sector and private sector pursued by India right from Independence with changing emphasis to suit the changing time appears to be most appropriate development model. This ensures the economy had the much needed cushion, comfort level and wherewithal to tackle any crisis situation.

In the years preceding global financial crisis of 2008, it is the public sector that came to the rescue of the government to deal with inflationary pressures arising mainly out of skyrocketing global oil prices, which at one time touched $147 a barrel. Huge losses were borne by public sector oil companies by not hiking the domestic retail prices and sharing a portion of the subsidy burden. Whereas domestic private oil companies closed down their petrol pumps. Public enterprises like Food Corporation of India, Central Warehousing Corporation, State Trading Corporation ensured that supply was not hit for the public distribution system. Public sector also contributed substantially to government kitty by way of taxes, levies and dividends. Statistics show that during 2007-08, when India clocked over nine per cent GDP growth for the fourth consecutive year, the central public enterprises contributed Rs 1.66 lakh crore, accounting for 23.6 per cent of government's revenue. This amount was nearly 12 per cent higher than the contribution in the previous year. Though private sector had grown in india particularly after economic liberalisation in 1991, the public sector contribution to the exchequer has not diminished in any big way and continued to account for more than one fifth of the revenue to the central exchequer. In States, the contribution of public sector is in no way less significant. Nearly one third of the annual business excellence awards instituted by CII-EXIM Bank have gone to public enterprises. Public enterprises did not lag behind private sector in the pursuit of business excellence and their contribution is noteworthy in all situations despite the fact that their shortcomings and hiccups get over amplified and that of private sector underplayed.

Post global financial crisis saw monetary and fiscal stimulus to kick-start the economy. This was to ensure proper utilisation of capacity created particularly in manufacturing. The public sector banks brought about financial stability in the country during the global financial crisis. The systematic and gradual reform of public sector banks since the liberalisation process held the banking system in good shape. This ensured that when the private sector banks had temporary stress during the global crisis in India, the public sector banks provided alternatives for customers and policy makers. India's major IT company, Sathyam, collapsed because of certain frauds. Likewise, global giant Enron collapsed for the same reason for indulging in unethical practices. But public enterprises provided a level of comfort and lend a helping hand to tide over the crisis. Some PSUs may not have performed well but overall the public sector banks and public sector companies provided much needed cushion and helped in stabilising the situation.

THE 2008 GLOBAL CRISIS HAD CONTAGION EFFECT ON INDIAN ECONOMY

The slowdown was graceful and soft and recovery rapid in India. Inflation was high and there was some foreign exchange depletion and large current account deficit accentuated by falling exports. But the situation stabilised quickly, and India back on road to recovery with macro economic stability with low and manageable inflation, low current account deficit and increasing foreign exchange reserves. All these augur well for the economy, which is one of the few islands of high growth, while several other economies including advanced nations are struggling to come to terms, seven years after the humongous crisis that struck the world. All global companies are looking up to India for investment opportunities while others were grappling with the difficult situation. India has now truly become the engine of global growth. The recent Corona Virus Pandemic has done some damage and certainly hurt the Indian economy just as in other countries. But the recovery is expected to be faster once the lockdown is lifted. Normalcy is expected to start only in the second half of this year and it is quite possible that financial year 2020-21will ensure India got back to pre-covid growth rate. Growth acceleration is expected only from subsequent year onwards. In this privatization of some of public enterprises like Air India and offloading of shares in Life Insurance Corporation will help in garnering some money through disinvestment. The Modi government's efforts to step up privatization and disinvestment process will have to wait until next year. The government has an ambitious plan to embark upon ending public enterprises dominance in some sectors to inject competition.

CHAPTER 9

Public Enterprises in States; Rate of Return Very Poor

The Eleventh Finance Commission in 2000 observed that the rate of return generated by public enterprises in states was close to zero and suggested that steps should be taken to ensure that they gave at least five per cent dividend on equity and 9 per cent interest on loans and advances.

The 1991 economic reforms launched had apparently not percolated to public enterprises in states unlike in the centre where public enterprises formed a crucial part of development strategy. India now as 28 states and nine union territories. While Telangana was carved out of Andhra Pradesh, Jammu and Kashmir state became two union territories of J&K and Ladakh to fulfil a long pending demand.

The poor rate return as in some central PSUs, pushed some states to gradually reform state enterprises just as it had happened at the centre to take on competition from private sector and foreign companies. But this process has been slow and tardy and perhaps much slower than in the case of central public enterprises.

Both central public enterprises and the state PSUs had taken firm root as they were set to build infrastructure and are in areas where private sector was not willing to invest as returns are not attractive. They were also set up to bring about price stability. The state public enterprises were nationalized once to protect the interest of sick industry or taken-over because of some malpractices. Initially state enterprises were basically state electricity boards for power generation, transmission and distribution. The state public enterprises gradually expanded into other spheres of activity over a period of time depending upon the requirement, which were different in different states. The State PSUs over a period of time are engaged in various activities including industrial development, finance, trading and marketing, construction services, consumer goods, engineering goods, development of backward regions and weaker sections just as central public enterprises. Some are involved in agro-industries, tourism, minerals and metals as well.

Electricity boards in most states are in bad shape because of the huge accumulated debt arising out of state government policy of not charging proper user charges. If free power is provided to farmers, the state government should subsidise fully the amount foregone but this does not happen impacting the health of discoms. Likewise municipalities do not charge appropriate user charge for supply of drinking water and other services rendered. State transport corporations, which subsidise travel when diesel prices shoot up to the detriment of the financial health of the transport corporations. They also provide free passes for students and senior citizens. Raising bus fares for both city travel and inter-city travel is difficult task for politicians as it is not a popular measure and suicidal in elections. So state administration usually allow state transport to bleed rather than take unpopular decisions. They do not subsidise free travel adequately as funds are required for other populist measures as well.

Practically all states have housing boards, which build houses for middle class, particularly lower. Some of them are run well and some are not. There are slum clearance boards, which too build houses for the slum dewellers. Nearly 50 per cent of state -run PSUs are commercial enterprises, which bring in revenue to state governments. These include engineering, electronics, textiles, mining, tele-communications, drugs and chemicals, sugar and cement. These were basically set up to prop up industrial activities using local resources.

4 STATES ACCOUNT FOR MAJORITY OF STATE PSUS

Four Indian states, Maharashtra, Gujarat, Karnataka and Andhra Pradesh accounted for 65 per cent of the total investments made in state level public enterprises (SLPEs) in India. This clearly indicated that states investing heavily in state level public enterprises have emerged as progressive states, a recent survey undertaken by department of public enterprises revealed in 2012 that out of Rs 2.9 lakh crore invested in SLPEs across 24 states till March 2008, for which the survey was conducted, Rs 1.9 lakh crore was invested only by those four states. Maharashtra with Rs 63,128 crore topped the list of investments, followed by Gujarat with Rs 52,137 crore. For the first time, such a detailed survey on investment, revenue, profit and loss etc. of SLPEs was undertaken.

Just after Independence, Madhya Pradesh and Maharashtra were ranked equal in many parameters. But Maharashtra chose to invest much more through its state enterprises and hence progressed much faster than Madhya Pradesh, which was until recently among the five BIMORU states—Bihar, Madhya Pradesh, Orissa, Rajasthan and Orissa.

SURVEY POINTS TO REGIONAL IMBALANCE IN STATES

The survey indicated regional imbalances in investments by states in their public enterprises needed corrective steps. The department of public enterprises has therefore decided to undertake capacity building programmes and impart special training to some state public enterprises to bring about parity across states. Both 13th Finance Commission and the erstwhile Planning Commission had expressed concerns in this regard. Unfortunately the data on state level public enterprises were not up to date. As of 2010 there were 849 state public enterprises across India. The reasons for survival and growth of state public enterprises are that it creates jobs in respective states. According to the survey, 55 SLPEs in Maharashtra alone employed 2.4 lakh people. Andhra Pradesh SLPEs engage 2.2 lakh people and those in Tamil Nadu employ 1.9 lakh.

PLANNING COMMISSION STUDY ON STATE PSUs

Planning Commission, which constituted a Study Group on Disinvestment of State PSUs in May 1999 came out with some startling observations about the state of affairs in public enterprises in states. The study group was headed by. N.J.Kurian, Adviser (Financial Resources), Planning Commission.

The study group felt that most of the State Governments set up the enterprises for job creation apart from propping up industrial activity. In some States, there is take-over as well from the private sector due to ideological bias. These States were Kerala, Tamil Nadu and West Bengal. Some States like Haryana, Karnataka, Kerala, Rajasthan and West Bengal treated these enterprises as vehicles of economic development.

The study conducted during 1985-94 showed that for most part of the decade, state enterprises collectively incurred losses. The losses high in the enterprises belonging to Andhra Pradesh, Arunachal Pradesh, Bihar, Mizoram, Nagaland, Uttar Pradesh and West Bengal. State PSUs of Haryana, Jammu and Kashmir, Karnataka, Maharashtra, Meghalaya, Orissa, Punjab and Tamil Nadu were having mixed performance, showing losses in some years and profits in others.

COMMERCIAL PSUS IN SOME STATES PERFORM BETTER

Commercial State PSUs of Gujarat and Madhya Pradesh earned not only a positive rate of return but also at the expected optimal rate of at least 7.5 per cent. State PSUs of Assam, Himachal Pradesh and Rajasthan earned a positive rate of return but far lower than the optimal rate of return of 7.5 per cent per annum on the capital employed.

A heavy concentration of these enterprises has been found in Andhra Pradesh, Assam, Goa, Gujarat, Haryana, Himachal Pradesh, Karnataka, Kerala, Maharashtra and Punjab. The maximum rate of return that these enterprises on an average earned during the period of this study was 1.62 per cent in 1987-88.

Commercial state enterprises in Bihar, Gujarat, Haryana, Karnataka, Maharashtra and Tamil Nadu recorded positive rates of return on their capital employed throughout the period of the study. The study puts the investment in State PSUs in 1996-97 at Rs.1,17,760.30 crore consisting of Rs.39,218.19 crore as equity and Rs.78,452.11 crore by way of loan. It also states that out of the total 1071 companies set up by State Governments, only 247 were profitable and 319 companies had eroded their paid up capital on account of persistent losses

About 80 per cent of the total investment in State PSUs in 1998-99 was shared by Andhra Pradesh, Delhi, Gujarat, Karnataka, Kerala, Maharashtra, Tamil Nadu, Uttar Pradesh and West Bengal. Delhi topped the table followed by Andhra Pradesh, Maharashtra and Uttar Pradesh.

MANY STATES HAD ACCUMULATED LOSSES IN THEIR PSUS

Over 90 per cent of the accumulated losses were incurred by Andhra Pradesh, Assam, Delhi, Gujarat, Karnataka, Kerala, Maharashtra, Orissa, Punjab, Tamil Nadu, Uttar Pradesh and West Bengal. Delhi and West Bengal were the loss leaders with Assam, Uttar Pradesh, Kerala and Tamil Nadu as their followers.

NO STATE EARNED BENCHMARK PROFIT BEFORE PROFIT AND INTEREST IN PSUS

Against the generally accepted norm of about 20 per cent of revenue earned, profits before interest and taxes for the State PSUs ranged from a high of 12.11 per cent in 1994-95 to 6.64 per cent in 1998-99. None of the States earned the benchmark profit before interest and taxes. Net profits should at least be equivalent to prime lending rate or 10 per cent of the revenue earned. However, the net profits for all the States taken together for the various years of the study excepting 1994-95 and 1995-96 were in negative. Net profits for all the States taken together have averaged around (-) 1.2 per cent of the total revenue earned over the study period.

As overall health of state level public enterprises, being not good, various steps were being contemplated. It included reform of public enterprises as at the centre, restructuring, disinvestment and so on.

Several states responded differently depending upon their own economic health, the political support to reforms in their respective states and the urgency and the realisation to improve state level public enterprises. There was also a feeling that enterprises that carried out welfare activities in the state should also be run on commercial lines or otherwise they should be converted into department. There was a demand to set up a social safety net to move towards smooth process of privatisation of state PSUs and a state renewal fund to be created by proceeds from disinvestment for restructuring state level PSUs. The performance of state level public enterprises improved more in those states which carried out more economic reforms.

After the erstwhile planning commission and finance commissions recommended reforms, state PSUs in several states started taking steps to restructure and reform to tone up their performance. They were however uneven. Despite problems, there was a general view just as in central PSUs, state level public enterprises have played important role in providing infrastructure services like power supply, road transportation and irrigation.

SECOND SURVEY ON STATE PSUs

The second national survey of state level public enterprises conducted by the Ministry of Heavy Industries and Public Enterprises in 2012 showed that there were 849 operating state level public enterprises in the country employing 18 lakh people.

Bulk of the investment in these enterprises has gone into infrastructure projects, which are mostly classified as public utilities. Out of the 579 enterprises, 357 SLPEs earned profits, while as many as 190 SLPEs incurred losses. Although these enterprises are often monopolies, they operate at a price disadvantage as they have to work under an administered price regime. Despite rise in inputs costs, prices of goods and services of these enterprises have not been correspondingly raised for years.

As high as 67 per cent of the investment in SLPEs has been in the power and energy sector, followed by investment in 'Industry' with a share of approximately 9%. Financial services claimed a share of 8%, comprising various promotional institutions catering to different sectors like handloom and handicrafts development, fisheries and forestry development etc. This was followed by investment in 'transport services' with a share of 5% of total (financial) investment. Sectors such as mining (4.5%), trading and marketing/other services (3.5%) and agriculture (2%) had comparatively much lower investments.

The total investment in the 579 SLPE's stood at Rs 3,29,079 crores. This comprised Rs 1,15,588 crores as paid-up capital and Rs 1,83,256 crores as long term loan. The debt-equity ratio accordingly worked out to 1.6:1.

State-wise, Maharashtra tops this list with a total investment of Rs. 63,129 crores followed by Gujarat, Karnataka, Andhra Pradesh and West Bengal.

The total turnover of the 579 SLPEs stood at Rs 2,39,453 crores. However, this figure does not give the true picture of the financial performance, as most public utilities, like power supply and road transport undertakings, are often required to operate under controlled/administered prices, much below the remunerative prices, which reduce the value of turnover.

In terms of gross sales/turnover, Gujarat topped the list with a turnover of Rs 42,038 in 2007-08. It was followed by Maharashtra (Rs. 35,725 crores), Andhra Pradesh, Tamil Nadu and Karnataka.

In terms of profit making SLPEs, Odisha led all the States with a net profit of Rs 2,232 crores. It was followed by Maharashtra (Rs 1,070 crores), Andhra Pradesh (Rs 1,053 crore), Gujarat (Rs 1,031 crores) and Karnataka (Rs 831 crores) The Orissa Mining

Corporation was also the most profitable SLPE posting a net profit of Rs 1,052.86 crores. Maha Genco (Rs 300.03 crores) and Maha Transco (Rs 258.20 crores) were the two companies from Maharashtra in the Top 10 profitable SLPEs l.

The survey also throws light on the most loss making SLPEs. Delhi Jal Board topped the list of loss making SLPEs with a loss of Rs. 1,567 crores. It was followed by Delhi Transport Corporation (Rs. 1,216 crores), Bihar State Electricity Board (Rs. 585 crores), Uttar Haryana Bijh Vitaran Nigam Ltd., (Rs. 495 crores) and Maharashtra State Road Development Corporation (Rs. 422 crore).

In terms of employment, Maharashtra topped the list, with a workforce of 2,44,625 employees in its 55 SLPEs. It was followed by Andhra Pradesh (2,27,889 employees), Tamil Nadu (1,97,206 employees), Gujarat (1,06,503 employees) and Uttar Pradesh (97,225).

One of the significant findings of the survey is that SLPEs, though burdened with several constraints contributed more to the exchequer by way of local taxes, value added tax and dividend pay-out, as compared to the subsidies they received from the respective state governments.

Sr.No.	**State**	**Contribution Exchequer (Rs Crores)**	**Subsidy Received (Rs Crores)**
1.	Andhra Pradesh	5944.97	4416.43
2.	Tamilnadu	4833.67	2282.85
3.	Kerala	4071.65	20.45
4.	Gujarat	2836.92	1566.38
5.	Delhi	2770.19	165.48
6.	Maharashtra	1383.56	646.70
7.	West Bengal	1378.04	303.97
8.	Orissa	1337.56	3.93
9.	Goal	180.05	3.57
10.	Rajasth		

It is clear from the survey that the industrially developed states of Western India and Southern India also have robust state level PSEs. An evaluation of the revenue and profitability of the enterprises also shows that wherever reforms have been implemented, the SLPEs have shown better results. In case of power utilities, for instance, collection of revenues has gone up significantly in states that have adopted franchising model.

Though India is a federal structure, a common pattern has evolved in public enterprises over a period of time, be it at central or state levels. These are basically departmental undertakings, public corporations and government companies. Also the operations of public undertakings range from the distribution of milk to the manufacturing of hi-tech equipment. The biggest problem faced by state level undertakings in India is the dilemma of balancing the requirements of control and the exigencies of autonomy. This challenge is common to all states in the country. With the 14 finance commission giving more financial autonomy to state and increasing states untied share, perhaps some of state level undertakings may get more resources and consequently more autonomy perhaps to run the enterprises on commercial lines. With the financial health of many states improving ever since 12th finance commission recommendations, only states like Kerala, West Bengal and Punjab are debt ridden. All the other states are better off financially. Now after special package to these states in the 14th finance commission, these states too would come out of the red in coarse of time. This indicates that states now have financial muscle to run them well. Of course the states' DISCOMS (electricity distribution companies) are still in huge debt in practically all the states. This is because of states not fully moving towards levying proper user charges. With centre now moving vigorously to reform this area, there could be some improvement in this area as well.

Now it is for Niti Aayog to work out a strategy for state-level public enterprises. In fact the Niti Aayog's plates are full in the sense they have to first deal with central public enterprises, which are privatised or divested of government shares before coming out with a strategy for state public enterprises. However there cannot be a one size fits all strategy for state public enterprises and situation is different in different states. Also different industry needed different strategy. Ideally a case-by case approach will be more appropriate. The government's efforts to reform discoms, state power distribution companies, has not worked fully so far.

CHAPTER 10

Changing Approach to Public Enterprises with Changing Time Under Modi

Ever since Prime Minister Narendra Modi came to power in 2014, there has been a change in approach towards public enterprises. Rightly government decided to step up off-loading its shares in public enterprises besides looking at privatization of some of them including loss making Air India. Many of the public enterprises had outlived its utility and needed drastic reforms. Privatisation is an answer but it is certainly not going to be an easy task. Modi government has the political will to do it and only time will tell how many public enterprises are privatised in the remaining four years of his present term in Modi 2.0.

The BJP led Vajpayee government pursued strategic disinvestment during 1999-2004 in Bharat Aluminum Company (BALCO), Hindustan Zinc (both to Sterlite Industries), Indian Petrochemicals Corporation Limited (IPCL) to reliance industries and VSNL to the TATA group. There were many more companies including some ITDC hotels.

Between 2014-2018, Modi government stepped up disinvestment to garner Rs 1,96,646 crore. This included minority and majority stakes of profitable public enterprises. It has subsequently decided to strategically disinvest in 24 public enterprises including Air India, which has accumulated loss of about Rs 70,000 crore in about a decade. This however did not go through in the face of corona virus pandemic, which had slowed down this process. It is expected to gather momentum in the post corona virus lock down period.

GOVERNMENT TO PRIVATISE PUBLIC ENTERPRISES IN NON-STRATEGIC SECTORS

The Modi government has taken an historical decision in May 2020 that government will privatise public enterprises in all non-strategic sectors. Besides, the number of Public enterprises will be limited to four in strategic sectors and any number beyond it will be privatised. The new policy announced by Finance Minister Nirmala Sitharaman aimed at pushing economic growth in post lockdown period. The details are yet to be worked out but this is seen as an attempt by Prime Minister Modi to instill confidence that government will do everything to kick-start the economy besides take measures to narrow the fiscal deficit due to falling tax revenue. This will also unlock value in central public enterprises, which are worth over Rs 10 lakh crore as per conservative estimates. BJP's trade union Bhartiya Mazdoor Sangh and Swadeshi Jagaran Manch have however opposed the move, which is expected to blow over once the details are spelt out.

The significant aspect is that all sectors will be opened up to private sector, besides it will unleash a wave of consolidation, mergers, divestment and privatisation. Once this drastic policy is detailed, there will be a lot of churning in the industry, which can only do more good than harm.

ALL SECTORS WILL BE OPEN TO PRIVATE INVESTMENT INCLUDING FOREIGN

The development is unique as it is for the first time an outright push for privatization is being attempted. It probably gives a push to Modi's idea of minimum government and maximum governance. But, privatisation is easier said than done as it can be a political hot potato.

Modi 1.0 mopped up Rs 2.8 lakh crore through disinvestment upto March 2019. In 2020-21, the budget has pegged disinvestment target at 1.20 lakh crore. The disinvestment target of 1.05 lakh crore was not achieved 2019-20 and it is not going to be different in 2020-21 too in the face of downturn due to lockdown.

IF NEHRU BUILT TEMPLES OF MODERN INDIA, VAJPAYEE DID ITS REFORMS

If Pandit Nehru was instrumental in taking Public enterprises to commanding height, Vajpayee laid the foundation for public sector reforms. Vajpayee first disinvested 26 percent of Hindustan Zinc Limited (HZL) equity through a strategic sale in 2000. He privatised 12 public enterprises including profitable Maruti Udyog, Bharat Aluminum, Videsh Sanchar Nigam Limited (VSNL) .Sterlite industries which took 26 per cent stake HZL, bought additional19 percent stake in November 2003 taking its share to 45 percent for around Rs 769 crore. A tottering company has now become the second largest Zinc-Lead miner and top 10 silver producer. Government still retains a 30 percent stake in HZL, which is worth much more than Rs 769 crore now.

Maruti is another success story. This controversial residual stake was off-loaded in May 2007. This Indo-Japanese partnership has now become a great Make in India case study.

TIME TO MONETISE HUGE LAND PARCEL WITH PSUs

Government is estimated to own at least 13,505 square km, nine times the size of Delhi. It could be more as the land data is yet to be completed. Even loss making Air India owns huge property, which has been separated before its hive- off. Government Land Information System (GLIS), a first-of-its-kind centralised database, created by electronics ministry, is still collecting data. This job is monitored by the Prime Minister's Office (PMO). This portal indicates the railway is the biggest landowner with 31,063 land parcels spread over 2,929 sq km. Defence ministry has so far uploaded data only 383.62 sq km of its total land assets but a 2011 Comptroller and Auditor General report puts defence land holding at 7,000 sq km. Many central and state public enterprises are yet to share their land details.

Vijay Kelkar committee in 2012 had recommended monetising the government's un-utilised and under-utilised land to finance infrastructure projects in urban areas. Maharashtra and Gujarat have since raised money by leasing out some of its land to the private sector.

MODI GOVERNMENT PLANS TO SELL SICK PUBLIC ENTERPRISES LAND

Many sick textiles mills which were closed down sold their land in prime locations in Mumbai and elsewhere in the country and massive real estate development had taken place in those lands unlocking huge value. Taking cue from it Modi government plans to dispose of the land of sick and loss making central public enterprises. The work has already started in case of Air India. Government is eager not to commit past mistakes of selling public enterprises along with the land parcel as it happened allegedly in the case of Modern Bread and VSNL.

A sub-committee headed by public enterprises secretary is reviewing the guidelines for land disposal. First, unused land is proposed to be disposed, mainly for government's housing for all programme. The land data bank, indicates, land for developmental purposes is available adequately for both agriculture and infrastructure development. Central government, state governments and public enterprises acquired huge amount of land soon after independence for developing industrial infrastructure, industries, ports, roads and railways, especially in backward areas but a large chunk of it had remained unused even today. In Lutyens Delhi alone, huge land parcel is with government, which had not been fully and properly utilised. That is true of other large cities in the country. According to 2012-14 public enterprises survey 2.35 lakh acres of surplus land is available with 58 under-performing CPSUs which have faced losses of Rs 56,845 crores, According to erstwhile Planning Commission in 2002 that only 53.6 per cent of the developed plots for industrial activities, were occupied. Special Economic Zones too have large parcel of unused land. There is huge vacant land with central ministries, including Defence, Railways and Civil Aviation. NITI Aayog, which was set up after dismantling planning commission by Modi, is reportedly working out a detailed master plan in this regard. Industry department is reportedly trying to sell 60,000 acres of idle salt land in various parts of the country to public enterprises. Five major states, Maharashtra, Andhra Pradesh, UP, Rajasthan and Gujarat acquired 572,793 acres for setting up industries but 45 per cent of it, 255,471 acres, has not been allotted to any industrial project. These lands were acquired for industrial corridor projects.

PSUs HAVE HUGE CASH SURPLUS: UTILIZED TO MEET DISINVESTMENT TARGET

Central Public enterprises had a cash surplus of nearly Rs 2.7 lakh crore in 2013-15. This cash surplus was mounting as fresh investments were not forthcoming due to excess capacity. By 2017-18, this had come down to Rs 1.7 lakh crore as this money was utilized to meet disinvestment and fiscal deficit targets by making cash-rich public enterprises to buy back shares and pick up stake of those PSUs that are being off-loaded through cross-holding. Indian Oil Corporation led the buyback rally during the year acquiring shares worth Rs 4,435 crore, followed by ONGC (Rs 4,022 crore), BHEL (Rs 1,628 crore), NLC (Rs 1,249 crore), Oil India (Rs 1,085 crore), Coal India (Rs 1,050 crore), NMDC (Rs 1,000 crore), HEG (Rs 750 crore), NHPC (Rs 600 crore) and National Aluminium Corporation (Rs 505 crore). PSUs have been made to pay higher dividends as well to meet the fiscal deficit targets. This has further strained PSU balance sheets. Coal India's interim dividend of Rs 8.132 crore was the highest followed by ONGC's Rs 8,021 crore, Indian Oil's Rs 8,060 crore. Power Grid Corporation and NTPC paid out Rs 3,050 crore and Rs 2,950 crore, respectively.

While increasing dividend payouts and share buybacks have helped the government meet its divestment target of Rs 80,000 crore in FY19, it has thwarted the companies' plans for higher capital expenditure with the economy picking up. Power Grid, being a prime example, has decided to scale down its capital spend to Rs 18,000 crore in the current fiscal from Rs 25,000 crore last year. In the HPCL deal, ONGC's cash reserve has been depleted and has been forced to borrowing hitting its bottom line. Government asked ONGC to buy its 51 per cent stake in HPCL, mopping up Rs 36,915 crore and exceeding its annual disinvestment target of Rs 80,000 crore for the first time. This eroded ONGCs cash reserves. In 2017-18, Power Finance Corporation (PFC) drew 70 per cent or Rs 10,150 crore from its 'reserves and surplus' to carry out the Rs 14,500-crore buyout of REC. Reserves and surplus were Rs 37,221 crore. While ONGC funded the acquisition through short-term debt and internal resources, the financial metric in the case of PFC was not as strong as that of the former. The surplus cash of PFC dwindled from about Rs 3,500 crore in FY17 to Rs 550 crore in FY18 after it paid a handsome dividend of 78 per cent of its paid-up capital in line with the government's rules. During the first half of FY19, the cash and cash equivalents in the balance sheets of PFC and REC were Rs 1,799 crore and Rs 22 crore. PFC has now been asked to bailout state discoms to enable them pay their dues to power generating companies. Cash-rich firms included BHEL, ONGC, BPCL, GAIL, Power Grid, NHPC, REC.

NEW POLICY ON PUBLIC ENTERPRISES – MODI'S REFORM AGENDA

Modi's new policy for public enterprises announced in May 2020 is aimed at accelerating growth in the post lockdown period so as to move towards $5 trillion economy. As per the new policy, the government will privatise all PSUs, except four in each of the strategic sectors.

Though the government may witness some road blocks, Modi certainly aims to make virtue of this reform measure. The 1991 reforms made it clear that privatisation is the way to go forward and there is room for the government to exit businesses where the social contract is minimal. These include tourism, hotel industry, consumer goods manufacturing, automobiles and such sectors where private players can provide consumers with abundant choice. But 30 years down the line, this aspect of reform agenda has remained unfulfilled.

Experience shows that government ownership has failed to deliver particularly in service sector and reasons could be many. A very good example is Air India. Civil aviation is a sector where companies operated on thin margin and hence there has to be hire and fire in-built into the system. In the early stages of development, there was need for government to own companies in this sector for security reasons and rightly private airline industry was nationalised and Air India was one of the top international airlines in the initial years. At that point of time most countries' flag carriers were owned by government. Today it is no longer the case. With thin margin of profit, airlines can be successful only if non-core activities are outsourced to experts in those areas. In case of Air India that is not the case. For example a permanent sweeper employee in Air India with say 30 years experience will be earning perhaps more than a junior pilot in a private airline as his salary would have gone up year after year besides substantial hikes in wage revision awards. The question, therefore, arises is: is it worthwhile to appoint such heavily paid sweepers. Also it becomes difficult to take work out of such highly paid sweeper as he would have become too senior and perhaps a trade union leader. Also he may not be in a position to retrain himself to operate modern equipment used for cleaning. Labour law may not permit such unsustainable labour force to be sacked. There are many such examples in public enterprises as one of the prime objectives in the initial stage was to provide employment besides development of backward area. The technology available then was also labour-intensive.

Modern bread was rightly set up as a public enterprise in an era of shortage to stablise prices and increase supplies. Today such intervention was not necessary with surplus food production and hence government has rightly exited.

Food Corporation of India was established for orderly procurement, storage and public distribution of food grains during a period of shortage. Today it has outlived its purpose and should therefore be restructured, reformed or even wound up as has happened in many countries. Setting up of FCI was a necessity in the 1960s and now it's a burden. Instead, what the country needed now was small and adequate storage facilities at district and taluk levels. Perhaps different types of storage like cold storage for perishables, dry and closed storage for food grains and cotton and so on. With APMC being dismantled, dispersed storage is more important than bulk huge storage near food grain production centres and ports. This increases transportation and other logistics costs, damage to stored crops, carrying costs, leakages and pilferages.

Of course there is no one-size-fits-all solution to overcome inefficiency in public enterprises. It had to be case-by-case approach. Like in the private sector, there are laggards and leaders in public sector as well as winners and losers. Each PSE has to be treated as a corporate entity with a balance sheet that does the talking honestly; no bookkeeping wonders.

Air India failed to attract a right suitor last time it was put up for divestment. Now, it is on the radar again. The government, which floated an Expression Of Interest in January 2020, has proposed to sell 100 percent stake in the airline along with entire shareholding in AI Express and 50 percent in ground handling joint venture—Air India-SATS. The EOI timeline was extended until June 30, 2020 and now further extended due to lockdown till August end.

It is not a good idea to sell only loss making public enterprises. Even profit-making should be sold to make them efficient and monetise assets. The government should be in the business of governance and not running business. In the early stages of independence, government had to step in as private sector was not forthcoming. It also did not mean government should not set up any public enterprises in future. If situation arises, it ought to step-in. A good example of recent times is Metro rail development. If private sector is not forthcoming to set up metro rail in many cities under public-private partnership, then government ought to step in for public good and many state governments in partnership with the centre have precisely done that. Public-private partnership has not worked well so far in this area. If it worked in future, government can exit or handover some of the future projects to them.

TIMING OF DISINVESTMENT AND PRIVATISATIION

To choose the right time for divestment is always a difficult task. Privatisation is even more difficult. With divergent political views in the country, it is always difficult get political consensus for public enterprises. If stock markets are consideration for deciding the timing, then there is no good or bad time. Due diligence in a transparent and accountable manner by experts is critical for disinvestment or privatisation. Opposition parties are always critical of disinvestment and left parties in particular will never allow disinvestment or privatisation as it is against their political ideology. Sometimes the intent of disinvestment of a particular company is of suspect. As far as possible market players should be kept out of disinvestment. Government should also fix realistic targets for disinvestment. Successive governments have failed on this score as year-after-year, the disinvestment targets in the budget have not been met. Some years, the government has come close to it. It is time that the targets are set realistically. Ideally, disinvestment, strategic sale and privatisation should be done under direct supervision of Prime Minister's office, so as to ensure transparency and accountability. It will also ensure prime minister of the day is held responsible.

POLITICAL WILL IS CRITICAL FOR PRIVATIZATION AND STRATEGIC SALE

Only time will tell If Modi has the political will. But if there is any Prime Minister who can muster political will, It is Modi. The guidelines of PSU reform policy announced in May 2020, will spell out how seriously government is committed to disinvestment, strategic sale and privatisation.

The UPA government under Manmohan Singh came out with some good proposals but it did not have the courage to implement them. To illustrate this point: the UPA Cabinet decided in 2005 to disinvest 10 percent in public sector power major, Bharat Heavy Electricals Limited (BHEL). But the decision had to be kept in abeyance because of opposition from its ally Left parties. Another attempt was made to disinvest BHEL during UPA 2. This time it was kept on hold because BHEL withdrew its draft red herring prospectus.

Modi government is committed to increased private partnership in Indian Railways, sell 100% stake in Air India, and attempts to disinvest oil and gas companies like Bharat Petroleum, SAIL, Shipping Corporation of India (SCI), THDC India, and NEPCO among others. Government is also committed to bring structural changes at least in seven sectors to encourage increased participation of private players. These sectors, dominated by Maharatnas, Navratnas and Miniratnas, include agriculture, coal, minerals, defence production, aviation, space and atomic energy.

WHY PRIVATISATON OF PSUs GAINING GROUND

Public enterprises usually is less efficient than private sector counterparts, in competitive markets as most of them operate with one hand tied down in view of bureaucratic and political controls. Some exceptions are always there. One reason is believed to be job security. There is also misuse of resources. Also overheads are usually higher in public enterprises compared to private sector.

Modi government gave in-principle approval for strategic disinvestment of central public enterprises including Air India, Pawan Hans and BPCL following the 2019-20 budget. These have not taken off so far as Lockdown came in the way. Now a new PSU reform has been announced but guidelines will take some time.

Take the case of Air India: If a private company can have more passenger flying miles than Air India, with the same number of planes, staff, buildings and managers, then there is something wrong with public enterprises. This is one way of measuring productivity. The sale of Centaur Hotel by NDA-1 when Arun Shourie was the disinvestment minister was guided by this logic. Instead of putting money year after year into a loss-making public sector hotel, the government was better off if the hotel was removed from its balance sheet. This applies to company like Air India as well.

MONOPOLY PSUs

Monopolistic public enterprises usually make profits and government can either continue to operate such companies or privatise after putting in place a system to regulate it. An example is setting up of

Airports Economic Regulatory Authority. Some of the airports are run by private companies now. Six airports were privatised 2019 and six more are to be privatised in 2020. Some 20-25 airports are to be privatised in the near future. Earlier some major airports like Delhi, Mumbai, Bengaluru, Hyderabad were privatised. Subsequently some more like Kolkata and Chennai were handed over to private players to run them.

PRIVATISATION IS HARD TO SELL POLITICALLY

Former British Prime Minister Margaret Thatcher's historic divestment campaign in the 1980s too saw political resentment but she successfully defended her government's strategy saying it was aimed at improving efficiency and longer-term growth. Thatcher was first to start this process. Modi too face some stiff opposition including some within the BJP party. But difficult economic situation helps in pushing reforms. The best example is that P V Narasimha Rao, who utilised balance of payment crisis to push through far-reaching economic reforms in 1991. India has not looked back since then. But BJP leader Subramaniam Swamy, who himself an economist and had some contribution to make in 1991 reforms, feels that Thatcher had a comprehensive plan to back her move including tax sops. But Modi has not so far backed his privatization move with such comprehensive plan.

The Modi government has reportedly want to rise the share of disinvestment receipts to 7 per cent of GDP from the present less than 2 per cent. This is a tough ask. The big ticket proposal is Life Insurance Corp. of India, or LIC and is expected to rake in as much as Rs 900 billion. The insurer major has more than a million agents and 300 million policies, together with stakes in hundreds of other companies. LIC stake sale may not go through all that easily and may require deft handling by Modi. The government will have to start the disinvestment process with a minority stake sale and certainly not attempt privatisation in one go in 2020-21. The public enterprises, which can be privatised and resort to strategic sale in 2020-21 could be Shipping Corp. of India Ltd, the nation's largest sea-cargo carrier, construction equipment maker BEML Ltd and Container Corp. of India Ltd. Bharat Petroleum earned a little over 76 billion rupees last fiscal year. The $7.4 billion sale of remaining government stake in Bharat Petroleum is expected by September, with some big Middle East oil producers and Russia's Rosneft PJSC are among the interested parties.

There are 10 Maharatnas PSUs, 14 Navratnas PSUs and 74 Miniratnas PSUs as on October 2019. There are nearly 300 CPSEs (central public sector enterprises). The government has decided in 2019-20 to divest its equity in most of these public enterprises to mop up Rs 3.2 lakh crore. Now In May 2020 the Modi government has announced a big ticket PSU reform to privatise in all non-strategic sectors and reduced the number to four in all strategic sectors. With further liberalization of foreign investment regime including up to 74 per cent FDI through automatic route in defence, only time will tell in the post lockdown period how the private players and multinationals respond. The huge land parcel and cash reserves of public enterprises would make them attractive and help government to unlock value. If Narasimha Rao- Manmohan Singh combine is still remembered for 1991 economic reforms, Modi will be remembered for big ticket privatization, if it goes through before the 2024 general elections. Statistics show Modi has mopped up almost double that of what Manmohan Singh garnered in his 10 year rule. During the 2014-2019 period, the government raised Rs. 2,79,622 crore from the disinvestment of public enterprises, compared to Rs 1,07,833 crore collected during 2004-14. According to the economic survey, the functioning of PSEs in India is limited by the need to report to a large number of different administrative ministries. So, the wishful thought of building a sovereign investment arm remains to be a challenging dream in the Indian context. Even after a long period of reforms, the Chinese SOEs still seem to be highly over-leveraged and structurally less efficient than their private-sector counterparts. World over public enterprises suffer from the inability to exercise authority. It is more so in the present day situation. It is true, that some of the loss making public enterprises, have turned around in

India but still they are not the most efficient in a competitive environment as public enterprise boards are not fully independent and professional. Along side hiving off public enterprises, public enterprises in India with its mammoth infrastructure could develop start-ups using their unspent resources. They can open their premises for fresh thoughts and new technology. Hindustan Aeronautics Limited (HAL), Bharat Electronics Limited (BEL), BPCL and Oil and Natural Gas Company (ONGC), are already supporting the government's 'Start up India' initiative, a collaboration that is mutually beneficial. Along PSU reforms, labour reforms too would have to go hand-in-hand for the Indian economy to revive rapidly post lockdown and Corona Virus pandemic to get back to high growth trajectory. If Modi succeeds in privatization of public enterprises, especially Air India and LIC, it will certainly be a feather in his cap and history will certainly record it.

About the Author

K.R. Sudhaman is a veteran journalist with over 45 years of varied experience. Sixty-eight year old Sudhaman is presently free lancing and writes in various economic and political issues after spending most of his career in India's premier news agency, Press Trust of India. An editor of repute, Sudhaman has extensively travelled with Prime Ministers of India on domestic and foreign tours including bilateral and multi-lateral visits. He has covered Indian Peace Keeping Force operations in 1980s in northern and eastern Sri Lanka and Mumbai's 26/11 terror attack. He has had two tough postings in Beijing, China, and Islamabad, Pakistan, during critical times. This included capture of Kabul by Taliban, fall of Benazir Bhutto government in 1996 and election of Nawaz Sharief in early 1997. He has covered Parliament for nearly three decades and that included interesting debates on Bofors, Mandal commission reports, Economic reforms in 1991, Downfall of Deve Gowda, in 1997, I. K. Gujral in 1998 and Atal Bihari Government in 1998. Apart from covering various global conferences of World Bank-IMF, G-15, G-8, WTO, EU and Women's conference, Sudhaman has served for over a decade as PTI's Economics Editor in Delhi and Western region Editor in Mumbai.